THE INCREDIBLE UPSIDE-DOWN FIXED-INCOME MARKET

Negative Interest Rates and Their Implications

Vineer Bhansali

CFA Institute
Research
Foundation

Statement of Purpose

The CFA Institute Research Foundation is a not-for-profit organization established to promote the development and dissemination of relevant research for investment practitioners worldwide.

ISBN 978-1-952927-18-8

Biography

Vineer Bhansali is the founder and chief investment officer of LongTail Alpha, LLC. His 29-year investment career started at Citibank, where he founded and managed the Exotic and Hybrid Options Trading Desk. He later joined Salomon Brothers in its Fixed Income Arbitrage Group followed by Credit Suisse First Boston in its Proprietary Trading Group. Dr. Bhansali was then at PIMCO for 16 years, serving the last 8 years as managing director and head of the Quantitative Portfolios Team, which he founded in 2008. He is the author of four books on finance, including *Bond Portfolio Investing and Risk Management* and *Tail Risk Hedging*, and has written more than 30 refereed papers on topics from option pricing to asset allocation in such leading journals as the *Journal of Finance, Financial Analysts Journal,* and *Journal of Portfolio Management*. Dr. Bhansali has received numerous awards, including the Graham and Dodd Scroll Award, and serves on the investment committee of the Margaret A. Cargill Philanthropies and on the board of trustees of MSRI and the Q Group. He holds a BS and an MS in physics from Caltech and a PhD in theoretical physics from Harvard University.

Acknowledgements

When I was first starting out in finance, I was tempted by all the dazzling new experiences: exotic options mathematics, traders' swagger, pontificating experts, you name it. But I was lucky to overcome it quickly, thanks to other travelers on the journey who had already experienced and figured out how to best deal with unpredictability and uncertainty. Working with investors who had developed the keen ability to see things as they really are and who understood how to implement ideas with common sense and finesse showed me, after numerous bumps in the road and the realization of mistakes, that much of what we read about the world of money and finance is really not that useful. I want to thank these many real and virtual mentors for the knowledge they have consciously and unconsciously imparted that has made an immense difference in how I think about investing and indeed about the world. Investing is a triply difficult profession not only because forecasting what the markets are going to do is close to impossible but also because forecasting what an investor might do under different moods and situations—and indeed what I might do under various situations—is difficult. Clear, independent, and commonsensical thinking are indispensable tools for the professional investor.

I would like to express my gratitude to all great practitioners in all fields who have shown the value of independent thinking, hard labor, and perseverance in chasing the truth and performance. Little do they know how they will continue to influence others, like me, in our own pursuits.

I would like to thank Larry Siegel for inviting me to write this piece and for his feedback and editing, Bud Haslett and his team at the CFA Institute Research Foundation for reviewing the manuscript, Steve Sexauer for helping draft the outline, and Chris Dialynas, Mike Ruetz, Kevin Schuyler, Ed Yardeni, Rebekah Bhansali, Roveen Bhansali, Rajasvini Bhansali, my colleagues at LongTail Alpha, and numerous other readers who would like to remain anonymous on comments on earlier drafts. This monograph has been written over a period of almost two years, and much has transpired in the interim in the world, economies, and the financial markets. As such, not all of the exhibits used in the monograph are from the same date. Fortunately, the points I try to make here are not impacted significantly by the lack of consistency in the data snapshots. Despite careful reading and editing, all errors and opinions are solely mine.

Dedication

To my family—Beka, Zane, Kieran, and Ara, and to my mother Vineeta, my sister Rajasvini, and my brother Roveen, and to the cherished memory of my father Rajendra Bhansali, who instilled the spirit of challenge and inquiry in all of us.

Contents

Foreword ix

1. Introduction: What Is All the Fuss about Anyway? 1
2. The Ongoing Debate about Negative Rates and
   Negative-Yielding Bonds... 6
3. Survey of Negative-Yielding Bond Markets 12
   Why Are Interest Rates and Bond Yields Negative?.......................... 21
4. Who Buys Negative-Yielding Bonds, and Why? 29
   Indexers and Passive Bond Exchange-Traded Funds 30
   Liability Hedgers 31
   Systematic Traders 32
   Speculators 33
   Arbitrageurs/Carry Traders.. 33
   Repo Use 36
   Central Banks 37
   Other Factors... 39
5. The Central Role of Central Banks... 41
   A Deeper Look at the ECB Monetary Policy 48
6. Consequences for Asset Valuation and Risk Management............... 62
   The Term Premium... 63
   Impact on the Stock Market 69
   De-Equitization: Buybacks and Stock Scarcity 72
   How Negative Yields Can Create Instability: The Rise
      of Shadow Financial Reinsurance.. 74
   Impact on the Banking Sector.. 78
   Impact on Derivatives Markets: The Resurgence of Equity
      Call Options 79
   The Rise of Digital Currencies.. 86
7. Conclusion: Is There Really Anything Wrong with Negative Yields? ... 88

Afterword: Between Here and the Long Run 92
Bibliography... 94
Disclosures 100

 **CFA Institute** This publication qualifies for 3.25 PL credits under the guidelines of the CFA Institute Professional Learning Program.

PL Qualified Activity

Foreword

The financial system as we have known it for many decades is dealing with a new reality of negative interest rates and yields. Behind this phenomenon lie many factors and their consequences that are important for every financial professional to understand.

In a levered financial system, central banks globally have had to ease monetary policy aggressively to keep their respective economies afloat. We know that bond market prices move in the opposite direction to yields. When yields are kept low, bond prices are mechanically increased. The lower the yield, the more rapid the rate of price increases. When yields become negative, as they have in Japan and Europe, the price of cash flows increases beyond any future redemption value. I have been warning of this phenomenon for several years now, only previously mischaracterizing it as a "Zika-like contagion" around the world when it should be updated to "COVID-19-like contagion."

I have had the pleasure of knowing Vineer for over 20 years now. He worked with me as a portfolio manager and head of analytics at PIMCO. In our time working together, we frequently discussed investment ideas and opportunities. In this monograph written for the CFA Institute Research Foundation, he analyzes the current state of the bond markets, the participants in the bond market, and what negative yields across much of the global bond markets could mean for investors.

Bond markets are possibly at a critical potential inflection point that will result in investors having to think of the ramifications of the current negative yields and the path of return to the more normal positive-yield environment sometime in the future. How will this affect economies and investors? While no one knows the future, investors must think about these issues carefully. In my view, this monograph is timely in bringing much-needed attention to this important topic.

Bill Gross

1. Introduction: What Is All the Fuss about Anyway?

> It seems fair to say, however, that the free market long-term rates of interest
> for any industrial nation, properly charted, provide a sort of fever chart of
> the economic and political health of that nation.
>
> —*Sidney Homer*, A History of Interest Rates

We live in a world of scientific experimentation and quick feedback, and it is fair to say that we are in the middle of a massive economic experiment whose ultimate scale and consequences are yet unknown. On balance, the dynamic of trial and error has been a very positive development for society. Experimentation is both a cause and a consequence of the ability and the willingness to take risk, and thus it depends on not only the right environmental conditions but also belief and, even more importantly, trust that regardless of how the experiment turns out, consequences will be mostly positive. Rarely in the history of mankind has trial and error, testing and failing, been such an important part of development. Indeed, much of the rapid development in the sciences can be attributed to the belief that taking exploratory risks is the right way to progress. Innovators in the tech industry live by the mantras of "move fast and break things" and "fail often and fail fast," attitudes that have led to rapid innovation and progress in the world we live in.

In financial markets, the environmental conditions that followed the global financial crisis of 2008–2009 led to an unprecedented economic and financial experiment in lowering yields below zero. The experiment is being performed in a laboratory called the global economy, and the experimenters are no less than a large group of highly educated PhD economists who help run our central banks. We truly hope that they succeed in their economic experiments because major errors can result in long-lasting economic scars. Forecasting the likelihood of the success or failure of this grand monetary–fiscal experiment is difficult, but imagining ways in which the outcome will affect the welfare of people is not. The rapid response can be credited for averting the global economy's fall into a prolonged depression even as recently as 2020, as COVID-19 brought the world to a standstill in a matter of weeks.

While the discussion of economic policy experimentation forms the backdrop for this monograph, and indeed for my very existence as an investor, exploring the phenomenon of negative interest rates around the world forces us to question some basic hypotheses. As of the writing of this monograph, almost 20% of the total market capitalization of the global bond markets is trading at negative yields (this ratio peaked at close to 30% in the third quarter of 2019). In other words, a buyer of these bonds, if she were to hold the bonds to maturity, will with certainty receive less than what she paid.

This is not a fleeting phenomenon, nor is it limited to a few exceptional countries. This phenomenon has persisted for close to half a decade in many regions, and signs are that it could persist for quite a while longer. The negative yield phenomenon is present in most northern European countries (Sweden, Switzerland, Germany, Italy, Portugal), in Japan, and even in Greece, which has a poor credit history! Dismissing this phenomenon as an "anomaly" that will correct itself with time would be too easy. Given how long negative rates have persisted in such countries as Japan, the distinct possibility exists that negative rates and negative bond yields could become the normal state of affairs in the coming decades. Could we look back with nostalgia at the days when bonds used to provide return from interest?

This question forces us to dig deeper into the meaning of the quote from Sidney Homer at the beginning of this introduction. If interest rates are a thermometer of the health of the nations we are considering, then low and even negative interest rates must mean that these nations have achieved Nirvana, which does not seem consistent with reality. But we cannot overlook that a key word in the quote is "free." To the degree that current interest rates are not a reflection of health but a result of policy that has been all too powerfully implemented by central banks, then the right analogy might be a thermometer in which the mercury has frozen to a targeted setting. What could be the motivation(s) behind this "manipulation," if calling it that is indeed fair? We will have plenty to say about this, while being careful not to ascribe a personal value judgment to policymaker decisions.

On a personal note, I should inform the reader that I was not trained as an economist. I was also not trained as an investor or a trader. I happened to accidentally pick up both as survival skills I needed to succeed in my job. I came with the ordinary intelligence of a person who was good at arithmetic and had the deep-seated desire to see things as they really are. While I have often failed to do so in the dynamic world of derivatives trading, I have also learned that coming at problems from principles and a clean slate allows one to look beyond dogmas. Logical analysis is the most potent tool we have in this time of unprecedented policy experimentation. I also think that economists and finance professionals have ignored, largely, the importance of each other's field, creating a fertile environment for investors to arbitrage the large-scale and consequential decisions made by economic policymakers and for policymakers to shake their heads each time financial speculation results in a bust that they have to mop up.

As the COVID-19 pandemic came out of nowhere and paralyzed the global economy, even the US Federal Reserve Board (Fed) went all in and slashed interest rates all the way back to zero in response to the precipitous fall in economic activity and stock market collapse, when only a year earlier, it was preparing markets for a gradual increase in interest rates. As of this writing, the Fed is still pushing back against negative interest rates in the United States, but forward interest rates have often traded below zero, and even short-term Treasury bills have traded at yields below zero for primarily technical reasons. But there is a distinct possibility that the next major crisis will force the Fed to go negative.

In Europe, investors have essentially gotten used to this state of affairs or have become conditioned to accept what might be called the "normalcy of deviance." This term was coined by sociologist and author Diane Vaughan to explain two tragic space shuttle disasters. Normalcy of deviance signifies the condition in which "people become accustomed to deviant behavior to the point that they no longer see it as deviant. They no longer see what is clearly visible" (Vaughan 2016). This, in Vaughan's view, explains the Challenger space shuttle disaster, in which engineers simply got used to leakage and faulty O-rings until it was too late. What seems normal in the world of bonds today might or might not be anomalous. But more important than identifying whether or not it is anomalous is knowing the potential risks and benefits to the financial system.

The negative rate experiment is an extreme test of classical economic thought, which holds that "inflation is always and everywhere a monetary phenomenon in the sense that it is and can be produced only by a more rapid increase in the quantity of money than in output," as Milton Friedman (1970, p. 24) said. The assumption that is being tested in real time is that if the system has ample liquidity, the money will eventually find its way into the real economy, which will result in consumption and growth. And because theory posits that demand drives prices, eventually the regeneration of demand close to or above potential output should drive inflation up.

While this theory is open to criticism and testing, the consensus in markets and in much of the economic profession is that, so far, the tsunami of money has not been able to generate the desired levels of inflation consistently. Indeed, as of this writing, the European Central Bank (ECB) is reviewing its policies to identify what is going on with inflation and why the theory is not working. Perhaps it is just a matter of time. Or maybe something else is going on, such as measurement focused on the wrong quantities.

The purpose of this monograph is to provide an overview of the negative interest rate phenomenon in its many dimensions. We need to look at the history of interest rates, the economic theories and policies that have led us to the current economic situation, their impact on asset prices and asset allocation, the behavior of participants (buyers and sellers), and of course, social and economic consequences. Surprisingly, this phenomenon is not very well understood at all, either in academia or in practice.

I do not have a strong philosophical view on the costs or benefits of negative interest rates. It is through my experiences as a physicist, with a doctorate on quantum anomalies, and as an investor, trading derivatives professionally for almost 30 years, that I have realized that anomalies, once understood, present opportunities. The negative-yielding bond market is like finding an amazing set of phenomena that I first need to understand and then perhaps try to profit from (see Box 1, "The 'God Particle of Modern Finance'?" in a later chapter). Neither task is easy, given that markets operate and clear and that for every seller of a negative-yielding bond there is a buyer, so one or the other is making a mistake, at least in the short run. Or perhaps policymakers and economic participants are speaking different languages and, as the character played by Strother Martin in the movie *Cool Hand Luke* says, "What we've got here is failure to communicate".

To an option trader like myself, a negative-yielding bond closely resembles an option. First, a buyer has to pay a premium that decays to zero as time passes because a negative-yielding bond is bought at a price higher than par. Second, it creates an asymmetric payoff if the yields become more negative, and it does so in a nonlinear and convex fashion. Finally, if the bond is held to maturity, even if yields rise, the maximum loss is limited to the price paid in excess of the redemption value.

Because it looks like an option, walks like an option, and talks like an option, to me, a negative-yielding bond is an option. But an option against what event? Could it be an option against future catastrophic default (e.g., in Europe by peripheral members) or permanent depression and/or deflation? We will discuss this in detail in later chapters.

Understanding a phenomenon that has no historical precedent is doubly difficult because few tools have been developed to analyze this type of environment. Using existing finance and economic tools on this phenomenon can lead to conclusions that could at best be silly and at worst be seriously detrimental to our financial wealth. On the other hand, the potential rewards from understanding this phenomenon are huge, both intellectually and financially. If the negative interest rate phenomenon is the biggest distortion of the past half century in financial markets as our gut, which might be wrong, tells us, then the eventual unwinding of the distortion will be painful for many and profitable for some. As with the dot-com bubble and bust or the housing bubble and bust, if negative rates and yields have created asset price bubbles in stocks and bonds, then the consequences to the financial markets and the economy will be substantial if this status quo changes.

But that is not a foregone conclusion. It is entirely possible that we are actually witnessing the natural consequence of humanity coming to a stage of its development where interest on deposits will take the same walk down memory lane that the Walkman cassette player did a few decades ago. That we are at the end of multiple centuries of financial market dominance is just conceivable, and negative yields are an intermediate mechanism to reset the system.

In any case, when I left theoretical physics almost 30 years ago, I did not expect financial markets to give me the opportunity to think about such a massive and possibly profitable puzzle on such a grand scale. My intent in this monograph is to lay out many of the pieces of the puzzle for you to consider, and perhaps it will provide you with the same excitement, fun, and rewards that solving financial puzzles has done for me. Negative interest rates are quite literally the whale of the current financial system, and yes, this monograph is about that whale.[1]

Vineer Bhansali
Newport Beach, California
April 2021

---

[1]In 2016, the *Telegraph* reported that Herman Melville received a letter of rejection for *Moby Dick* asking whether the book had to be about a whale.

2. The Ongoing Debate about Negative Rates and Negative-Yielding Bonds

> The idea of negative interest rates may strike some people as absurd, the concoction of some impractical theorist. Perhaps it is. But remember this: Early mathematicians thought that the idea of negative numbers was absurd. Today, these numbers are commonplace. Even children can be taught that some problems (such as $2x + 6 = 0$) have no solution unless you are ready to invoke negative numbers.
>
> *—Greg Mankiw, "It May Be Time for the Fed to Go Negative,"*
> New York Times

Why would an economist advocate taking interest rates below zero? The main motivation is the foundational economic assumption that low interest rates stimulate aggregate demand. If the economy is falling into a recession, then by cutting interest rates, economy-wide borrowing costs should fall, lowering the cost of money and incentivizing consumers and businesses to spend more, resulting in growth.

This theory assumes a unidirectional causality that if the price of credit (i.e., the interest rate) falls, spending should increase. To take the argument one step further, the current central bank consensus, at least in Europe and Japan, is that if low rates are better, then there is no reason to stop at zero; "going negative" might further stimulate demand and therefore growth.

Other economists argue that the reality is not so simple, and recent data from experiments with negative rates have shown that the results are less than convincing: Negative interest rates do not necessarily stimulate demand. Indeed, some (Brunnermeier and Koby 2018) argue that below a certain rate ("reversal" rate), negative interest rates can throw sand in the works by hurting banks so much that they refuse to lend. If banks refuse to lend, money just gets clogged up at the banks, leading to investment in financial assets rather than loans for economic activity. Economists of the ECB estimate this reversal rate at approximately –1% (Darracq Pariès, Kok, and Rottner 2020), while the deposit rate of the ECB at the time stands at −0.50%.

The occasionally used counter to this counterargument is that the level of rates and the quantity of excess credit and money are not yet negative enough. In other words, in due time, and done in a large enough size, negative interest rates will indeed result in growth and inflation, which have become the key target metrics for central bankers. The primary example of this philosophy is the ECB, which has taken the view that "more for longer" (i.e., increased purchases of financial assets while keeping short- and long-term interest rates low) will eventually result in real growth and a rise in inflation. New ECB President Christine Lagarde has expanded her predecessor Mario Draghi's negative interest rate policies further, including recently announced preferential treatment and indirect financial subsidies for banks that participate in buying bonds with negative yields.

Many respected economists and former Fed governors have also argued vehemently for negative interest rates. Kenneth Rogoff (2020) has argued that

> For starters, just like cuts in the good old days of positive interest rates, negative rates would lift many firms, states, and cities from default. If done correctly—and recent empirical evidence increasingly supports this— negative rates would operate similarly to normal monetary policy, boosting aggregate demand and raising employment.

Rogoff continues,

> A number of important steps are required to make deep negative rates feasible and effective. The most important, which no central bank (including the ECB) has yet taken, is to preclude large-scale hoarding of cash by financial firms, pension funds, and insurance companies. Various combinations of regulation, a time-varying fee for large-scale re-deposits of cash at the central bank, and phasing out large-denomination banknotes should do the trick.

How will public opinion be managed? In papers that read like a manifesto for executing upon this set of "tricks," former Fed governor Narayana Kocherlakota (2020) as well as Ruchir Agarwal and Miles Kimball (2019) have laid out ways by which governments can take interest rates negative and manage the political repercussions of doing so by essentially making the problem one for the commercial banks to sort out. They echo the statement heard primarily from economists that "the zero lower bound is not a law of nature; it is a policy choice," further suggesting that

> Relying on banks for transmission of a negative rate of return on paper currency reduces the implementation burden and political cost associated with negative rates. When working through banks, anything that would be a political problem for the central bank becomes a customer relationship management problem for the commercial banks. Commercial banks are likely to be better and more experienced in dealing with customer relations problems—even those with a new twist—than central banks are at dealing with grassroots political problems. After minimalist implementation (at the central bank cash window), the central bank can leave the rest up to the

private sector. One key aspect of bank transmission approaches is that the less the central bank does and the more is done by commercial banks, the less new legislation is likely to be needed. (Agarwal and Kimball 2019, p. 4)

From the perspective of many market observers, this approach of making negative interest rates a problem for commercial banks to sort out is fatal for the banks and for the economy at large. For example, in reference to negative interest rates, the chairman of JP Morgan Chase, Jamie Dimon, said, "I think as a permanent part of policy it's a really bad idea" (Lee 2019). Another commentator says that "negative rates actually threaten the financial system" (Bianco 2019).

Even in academic circles, certain economists believe that below a certain level of rates, banks become less likely to lend. At this "reversal rate," low interest rate policy backfires (Brunnermeier and Koby 2018). To offset this aversion to lending, the central bank (e.g., the ECB) resorts to fixes that ensure bank profitability, such as "tiering" fees on deposits or even a persistent secondary market bid for assets. The BIS (Bank for International Settlements) has so far not been an all-in supporter of negative rate policies, warning in 2019 that "there's something vaguely troubling when the unthinkable becomes routine" (BIS 2019).

Lest the reader think that economists agree on the benefits of negative interest rates for the real economy, note that others argue, "In this framework we showed that negative policy rates were at best irrelevant, but could potentially be contractionary due to a negative effect on bank profits" (Eggertsson, Juelsrud, and Wold 2017). This quote expresses the view that negative rates can actually be worse for the economy than doing nothing.

Faced with these competing theories, no wonder both the public and investors are confused about what the right answer is. Should we support negative rates or not? At best, the public leaves the deliberations to economists, as long as the outcomes are not too nasty for the real economy and financial markets. At worst, the public realizes that if the experiment fails, severe financial market and economic damage would result, and people could start to prepare for it using precautionary reduction in consumption and economic activity.

Until more reliable evidence is gathered—which, unfortunately, can be done only through experience—the jury is still out on the efficacy of negative interest rates for improving *economic* outcomes over the medium and long term; we simply do not have historical precedent or data. However, enough evidence exists that negative interest rates have a direct and almost immediate consequence on *financial market* outcomes.

In other words, even though the main reason for the vehement belief in negative interest rates is the central bank desire to increase consumer price inflation, remembering my embellishment of Goodhart's law (1981) is worthwhile: "When a measure becomes a target, it ceases to be a good measure"[2] (for the thing it is trying to measure). Although headline inflation numbers are not meeting their target (yet), the massive increase in the availability of credit and money has certainly resulted in an increase in the price of financial assets. If negative rates in the short run result in the appreciation of asset prices, the wealth effect muffles out most complaints from those who own assets. However, increasing inequality between asset owners and members of the public that do not own assets creates a new set of problems that can be best described as a potentially explosive unintended social consequence of low and negative yields. We will pick these issues up again in the later chapter on consequences.

Another interesting aspect is the impact on paper money. If interest rates were to go substantially negative, at some point, the public would refuse to hold deposits at central banks that yield below zero. Instead, people would opt to hold cash or other assets. The government could run into a problem if the yield on deposits is negative but the yield on cash is zero. This is exactly what happened in April and May 2020 when the Treasury issued T-bills that were auctioned at zero yield but began to trade in the open market at negative yields as the massive amount of liquidity found a place to park. Do negative interest rates on deposits mean that physical, paper cash will have to be eliminated? Eventually, unless the government elects to have two simultaneous currencies, one electronic and one paper, the elimination of most paper money could indeed be the ultimate outcome of an extended negative rate policy. One way, as discussed by Buiter (2009), is that whenever the public wants to exchange physical paper cash currency for "real," electronic money, a transaction tax would be charged that would make the value of the paper money equal to that of the electronic money. In other words, a persistent negative rate environment will render the centuries-old tradition of paper bills ancient history. Perhaps the specter of this possibility, remote as it might be, has resulted in the resurgence of private, decentralized money such as bitcoin and the emergence of a large number of believers in digital assets as a store of wealth.

As discussed by Rogoff (2020), the government "taxing" money by putting a negative yield on it is no different from the inflation tax that it surreptitiously employs already. The tax will simply become explicit as the convergence

---

[2]This well-known description of Goodhart's law actually comes from Strathern (1997).

between "monetary" and "fiscal" policies becomes explicit and the Fed and the corresponding "Treasury" reenact an implicit coalition, coordination, or "pact" that Ed Yardeni calls the "T-Fed." In this setup, the Treasury borrows money by issuing bonds, and the Fed purchases those same bonds by printing money. Because the actions of both the Fed and the Treasury emanate from the objectives of government, historical episodes not surprisingly confirm that "the lines of authority between a Treasury and a Central Bank" can be ambiguous, obscure, and fragile (Bassetto and Sargent 2020).

The Fed and the ECB are currently privileged to have a monopoly on currency issuance within their regions. This enables them to print paper money, which, according to the Fed, costs approximately 12 cents per US$100 bill. In other words, the Fed realizes a "seigniorage profit," which is recycled to the US Treasury, of between US$50 billion and US$100 billion per year by issuing paper currency that relies on its credibility for its value, perceived or real. This seigniorage adds approximately 0.50% to US GDP every year. In Europe, the number might be slightly higher because of the greater number of cash transactions.

The ultimate beneficiary of this exorbitant privilege is the government because it can translate, by fiat, paper into something much more valuable. If negative rates mean that paper currency would have to be eliminated, that elimination would have substantial social impact. On the positive side, it would preclude a large amount of tax evasion and criminal activity that is done in cash (Rogoff [2020] estimates that one-half of the dollars and euros circulating outside the region of issue are used for such purposes). On the negative side, it would give governments carte blanche to reach into its citizens' pockets and levy a tax by giving them a negative yield or what is the same, less nominal money in the future.

Let me finish this introductory chapter with an example of one of the most successful investors of recent times in the context of the regime shift in yields. Warren Buffett's investment strategy relates long-term yields to his approach to long-term return generation, thus highlighting how deeply embedded long-term yield considerations are in evaluating strategic investment opportunities. In one of his letters (Cunningham 2019), Buffett gives a rationale for writing long-dated put options backed by the float of Berkshire. He assumes that Berkshire can sell 100-year expiry put options that, "using the implied volatility assumption for long-dated contracts that we do, and combining that with appropriate interest and dividend assumptions" (p. 269), result in a Black–Scholes premium for the contract to be 0.25%. To the naked eye, this seems like a very small "tail risk" premium, which most would be unlikely to take. However, Buffett, with his access to long-term capital and "float," argues that both inflation and the 100 years of retained earnings will hugely increase the value of most of the companies in the index.

He then goes on to argue that even if the probability of a large decline—of say, 50%—were to happen with a probability of 1%, the expected loss would be only 0.5%. So to make up for the loss, the initial premium would need to be invested at an annual yield of just 0.70%. He finishes the argument with the rhetorical question: "Would you like to borrow money for 100 years at a 0.7% rate?" (Cunningham 2019, p. 269).

When rates are closer to zero, however, rerunning this calculation with 0% yields would show that the premium received would not grow at all and would therefore be insufficient to face the obligations if the equity markets declined. If yields were negative, say –1%, the value of the premium would actually decline over time, losing more than one-half of its value. If the fall in the equity markets is associated with a fall in the reserve that this premium is expected to grow to, then the seller of the put will be severely underfunded. In other words, Buffett's conclusion that "either my assumptions are crazy or the formula (Black–Scholes) is inappropriate" (Cunningham 2019, p. 269) has to be given more thought in a world of low and negative yields, where the very concept of a risk premium is challenged.

The impact of this type of calculus is very important for strategies that generate returns from selling "insurance" and, by extension, for strategies that look to hedge future liabilities of pension funds and similar bodies. When yields are negative, the premium received today is not guaranteed to be sufficient to make up for the obligations if they were to come due. This means that to hedge liabilities, the writer of the insurance policy has to buy long maturity bonds, in the process of which, yields are driven even lower. This mismatch between assets and liabilities can make a large impact in the funded status of many public pensions, as has recently been the case. The mental exercise of comparing investment alternatives based on long-term yield is so central to all investment decisions that when yields are negative, many dearly held investment principles are upended.

As we can see, the negative interest rate phenomenon has consequences that influence almost every part of financial decision making. This is to be expected, given that the entire financial system is based on the idea of the time value of money. Any foundational change to this assumption can send tremors that have the potential of shaking all the structures built on this assumption. Let us take a quick survey of the bond markets of the day to get some clues.

3. Survey of Negative-Yielding Bond Markets

Few people ever actually saw a *Semper Augustus* flower. The man who held a near monopoly on the small supply . . . refused to sell his bulbs, which drove up the price. In 1638, one was advertised for 13,000 florins, the price of a nice house. That was the year the market for tulips in the Netherlands crashed.

—*Sarah Laskow, "The Most Beautiful Tulip in History Cost as Much as a House,"* Atlas Obscura

Debt has existed in one form or another for almost as long as humans have understood the time value of money (for an extremely long-term history, see Homer and Sylla 2005). The history of interest rates has been well documented for millennia, and governments in ancient, medieval, and modern times have used interest rates as a tool for achieving economic objectives.

Interest rates are, quite simply, the price of money (credit) for a given period. For you to lend me money for some duration (a few hours to 100 or more years), you must value all the pros and cons of this transaction, and unless you are a family member or friend, in exchange for the loan, you will require me to give you something. When converted to the standard unit of an annual rate for longer maturities, this compensation for temporarily parting with your money becomes what we call a "yield." Because the duration of the loan is a variable, the yield is a function of the duration that the money is lent for. These loans are made at different times and different maturities, so we can picture a "yield curve," which simply plots the cost of borrowing money against the amount of time before the loan has to be paid back. In addition to receiving the principal or the corpus of the loan at some maturity, investors also sometimes expect to be paid something in the interim. This is the "coupon" on the bond. A bond that pays nothing in the middle is called a "zero-coupon" bond.

Over time, and as the pricing and valuation of bonds matured, investors realized that rather than buying and holding bonds to their maturity, they could trade the bonds. This ability to trade bonds and their derivatives resulted in the existence of bond *markets*. For readers looking for more detail on bonds and their valuation, plenty of references are available on every aspect of the bond markets, including two by this author (Bhansali 2011; Wise and Bhansali 2010). While we refer here to bonds, cash is a special case of the bond market. We can think of cash as simply an instantaneous bond.

The size of the total global bond market in 2020 was approximately US$70 trillion, if we include only bonds that are in the widely followed Barclays Global Aggregate Bond Index for liquid bonds. Of course, other "bonds" exist as well, many of them private (e.g., "bail bonds" that keep one out of jail). My focus in this monograph is on the liquid bond markets.

While this monograph is being written, the financial markets are recovering from the impact of COVID-19, the coronavirus pandemic that has hobbled the global financial system and brought global economies to a correlated sudden stop. As a consequence, central banks globally have pumped massive, unprecedented amounts of liquidity into the financial system, essentially driving both short- and long-term interest rates to nothing, or even below nothing (i.e., negative).

But their actions are not the only reason we are living in unprecedented times. In a tightly bound ecosystem where investment strategies are linked to each other through feedback and arbitrage mechanisms, the low yields of government bonds have resulted in significant changes to the valuation calculus of all asset prices and indeed of portfolio construction. The reason for this monograph, then, is that almost 25%, or almost US$20 trillion, of these bonds have recently traded at negative yields (**Exhibit 1**). Global central bank balance sheets, not purely coincidentally, have also grown close to

Exhibit 1.   Market Value of Negative-Yielding Bonds in the Barclays/Bloomberg Global Aggregate Bond Index, 19 August 2015 to 6 August 2020

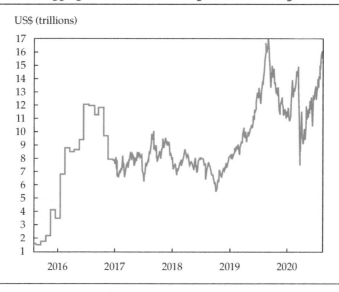

Source: Bianco Research, LLC. Used with permission.

US$25 trillion, and risky asset markets have seen a growth in dollar terms of the same magnitude over the period.

Negative-yielding bonds also affect geopolitics because geopolitics influence the bond markets. Anecdotally, on 17 November 2020, China's finance ministry issued €750 million worth of five-year bonds at a negative yield of −0.15% (Lockett and Hale 2020) and a price of €100.763. The redemption value of this bond at maturity will be €100. Considering that European investors at the time were faced with the reality of German bunds (the short name for Germany's sovereign bonds) trading at −0.74%, this yield pickup of almost 0.59% looked quite substantial. From the perspective of the Chinese government, the offering provided a unique and very easy mechanism by which it could diversify its vast reserve balance while getting paid to do so.

Considering the ongoing geopolitical tension between the United States and China, market participants have long expected China to reduce its dollar holdings and allocate them to Europe. By issuing foreign debt in euros at negative yields, the Chinese government can generate large inflows in euros and at the same time get paid for borrowing. Unlike other issuers of bonds in euros, China does not have to recycle the euros into negative-yielding euro deposits to hedge the currency risk. It can simply hold the euros as reserves.

Operationally, investors do not actually mail a check when they buy a negative-yielding bond because there is no coupon. The current price over par results in a negative yield because investors simply pay more at issuance than the amount they will receive in the future. To be exact, in the example used here, for every €100 that they will (hopefully) receive in five years, they are willing to pay a little over €100.75 today. The extra €0.75 is where the negative yield comes from.

Investors have also been looking for signs that the Chinese are diversifying out of their massive holdings of US debt that are held in Treasuries. So far, little, if any, sign of the sale of these Treasuries has been seen. That is just as well, because the first large tranche of Treasuries that is sold will be met by an anticipation on the part of the markets that more is to come, which could result in a huge impact on the price. With the Fed having adopted Modern Monetary Theory in all but name, the Chinese have another reason to rationally not sell their dollar bond holdings: The US taxpayer, via the Fed, is buying them at higher and higher prices, to the tune of US$80 billion–$120 billion a month!

A private enterprise could also issue debt in euros at negative yields, but once the euros were received, that enterprise would have currency risk. If the euro's value were to fluctuate, the enterprise could end up owing more real value in the future when it has to redeem the euros. Thus, a private enterprise would have to hedge using the currency market, and the act of currency hedging could negate a lot of the benefit of the low (negative) yields.

A sovereign does not have this same constraint; the Chinese government has the long-term goal of diversifying its currency reserves. So, holding euros and enduring the currency fluctuations are actually beneficial to the Chinese government and consistent with its diversification objectives. If the euro weakens over the redemption period, the Chinese will redeem them with fewer renminbi. If the euro strengthens, the government can simply print more renminbi to exchange for the euros needed.

From the perspective of a market participant, this is a form of brilliant global arbitrage. If every other sovereign with a printing press realizes that in the short term, you can get this "something" for "nothing," we can expect much more issuance of euro-denominated low- or negative-yielding bonds, an action that could ultimately result in more supply and less demand for these bonds. But the timing for such a saturation seems to be far away because the captive buyers (discussed in the next chapter) are a dominant portion of the growing bond market.

In almost 5,000 years of recorded history, we have perhaps seen no other instances in which such a large fraction of the bond market has traded with such persistent negative yields, but rationalizing the current status quo is becoming increasingly easier. Alan Greenspan has said that "zero has no meaning, besides being a certain level"—that is, there is nothing special about positive yields (Fitzgerald 2019). I will let the reader decide whether there is indeed nothing special about lending and getting paid for it or lending and paying for the privilege of doing so. Yields below zero do, however, turn the calculus of finance upside down because the interest rate term structure is one of the three most fundamental inputs used in today's framework for pricing financial assets.

The "fair" price of any asset is the probability-weighted (i.e., expected) present value of future cash flows. In other words, to price any asset, you forecast the future cash flow then discount that future cash flow by the interest rate. If the cash flow is deterministic, you are done. But if the cash flow is not known with certainty, you must average over all the possible outcomes based on the probability of that outcome occurring in the future, then discount that uncertain price to a present value by a yield reflecting that uncertainty, and finally average over all the possible present values to obtain the expected value. We can see how this process can become very complicated if the discount factor becomes inverted when yields are negative, given that the expected value received in the future is less than the value today.

The reason this state of affairs is amazing from a theoretical finance perspective is best explained with an example (see **Box 1**, "The 'God Particle of Modern Finance'?" at the end of the chapter for the importance of a negative yield, long-term, zero-coupon bond for financial analysts). In mid-September 2019, the German government issued a 31-year maturity, zero-coupon bond at a yield of −0.12%, or a price of €103.61 (DBR 0 08/15/2050), which became the benchmark 30-year bund. Because this is a zero-coupon bond, the only return of capital a buy-and-hold investor can receive is the €100 or redemption value at par in 2050. However, the buyer of this bund was willing to pay 3.61% above par value to receive par. In other words, the investor would pay a "premium" of 3.61% for a guaranteed return of principal. Assuming that the duration of the bond is roughly 31 years, this tells us that for each year to maturity, the investor on average is willing to part with approximately 12 bps of his or her capital per year. Why an investor might be willing to do this will be discussed at length in the next section.

The problem we face here is that if interest rates are negative, then the present value of the future cash flow is higher today than in the future. In other words, the time value of money is negative. To see this simply, note that if you have a bond that pays you a dollar at maturity T and has a yield of y, then its present value, or price P (assuming no coupons in the interim), is simply $P = e^{-yT}$. We can easily see that if the yield becomes more negative, the price today becomes higher and higher, at an exponential rate, than its future guaranteed principal of 1.

We can easily dismiss this observation as an anomaly of the bond markets. But because this exact same arithmetic applies to all asset pricing, we can see that negative interest rates could, in theory, make the price of all assets much higher, all else being equal. Does this matter? We will discuss this topic toward the end of the monograph. For now, just note that negative interest rates and yields "pull value forward," so anyone who buys these bonds and holds them to maturity will, with certainty, lose money in nominal terms.

In recent years, the percentage of negative-yielding bonds as a proportion of all bonds has increased dramatically. As of early January 2021, the total value of negative-yielding bonds was US$17.4 trillion. The total value of the Barclays Global Aggregate Bond Index was US$67.04 trillion. So far, the previous peak was in August 2019 at 30.2%, but at that time, the total outstanding in the Global Aggregate Bond Index was less, approximately US$55 trillion. Thus we can see that the significant increase in the market value of the total bond market reduced the percentage in negative-yielding bonds (**Exhibit 2**).

Exhibit 2.   Negative-Yielding Bonds in the Barclays/Bloomberg Global Aggregate Bond Index, as of 6 August 2020

A. Global Aggregate Market Value

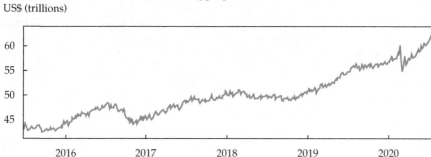

B. Negative-Yielding Global Aggregate Market Value

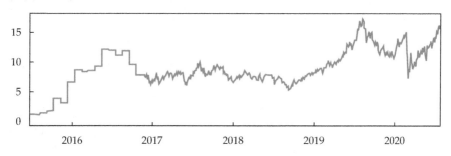

C. Percentage of Global Aggregate with Negative Yield

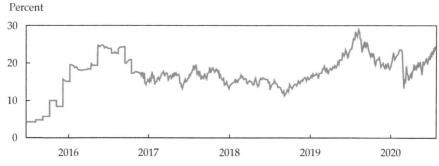

Source: Bianco Research, LLC. Used with permission.

Negative-yielding debt is currently a little over 25% of the total outstanding debt in the Barclays Global Aggregate Bond Index (as of early 2021). The option-adjusted spread of the negative-yielding debt is a measly 0.1565%, and the average maturity is 5.7 years. The average duration of the negative-yielding bond market is 5.39 years. So, the spread per unit of duration was below 3 bps, or 0.03% per unit of duration (**Exhibit 3**). This is a measure of

Exhibit 3. **Option-Adjusted Spread, Average Maturity, and Average Duration of the Negative-Yielding Bonds in the Barclays/Bloomberg Global Aggregate Bond Index, as of 6 August 2020**

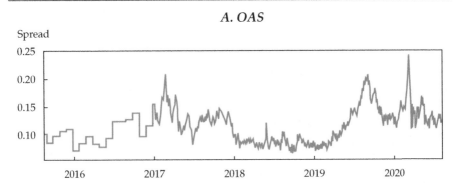

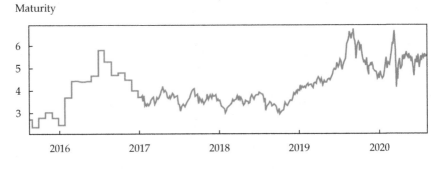

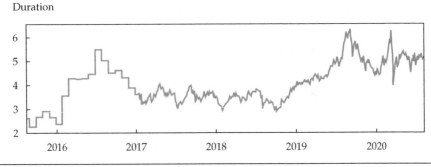

Source: Bianco Research, LLC. Used with permission.

risk that brings home the point that a very small rise in spread could wipe out all the spread income from the bond.

In terms of the geographical distribution and in terms of US dollar equivalents, US$4 trillion (23.6%) of negative-yielding debt is in Europe (with the exception of Germany and France), US$2.67 trillion (15.6%) is in France, US$2.69 trillion (15.6%) is in Germany, US$5.04 trillion (29.3%) is in Japan, and US$2.72 trillion (15.9%) is in the rest of the world (**Exhibit 4**). Surprisingly, so far, the United States has not entered the negative yield club.

By type of security, sovereign debt is US$12.5 trillion (73.2%), corporate bonds are US$1.25 trillion (7.4%), government-related debt is US$2.14 trillion (12.4%), and securitized debt is US$1.2 trillion (7%). So, we can see that even though the majority of the negative-yielding debt is government issued, there is a substantial amount of corporate debt (where the underlying corporation has the possibility of defaulting, of course with severe consequences), which is also at negative yields.

Note that even though nominal yields are positive in the United States, real yields in the United States have now plummeted to the lowest levels seen in recent memory as the Fed has slashed interest rates and bought assets. (Real yields were often negative in the 1970s as inflation raced ahead of nominal interest rates.) The Fed owns US$6.72 trillion of the US bond market, which is 26% of the total, excluding corporate and high-yield bonds, and it owns 30% of both the Treasury bond market and the mortgage-backed securities market. It has recently bought almost 20%, or US$318 billion, of the total Treasury Inflation-Protected Securities (TIPS) market and is now one of the largest holders of such bonds.

If real yields are a reflection of the state of economic growth, then the TIPS market seems to be pricing in 10 years of no real growth, or what is more likely is that the Fed-driven buying of TIPS has created this mirage of no real growth (**Exhibit 5**). A closely watched statistic, the so-called break-even inflation rate, is the difference in yield between a nominal Treasury bond and the real yield on a TIPS bond of equal maturity; this is widely considered a market measure of expected inflation, but currently it is at least partly controlled by the Fed through its asset purchases. In other words, the information content of the breakeven inflation rate as a measure of expected inflation is impaired because it is currently highly influenced by Fed actions. In Switzerland, Germany, the Netherlands, Denmark, and Finland, nominal rates were recently negative all the way out to 30 years.

The effect of purchasing negative-yielding bonds until very recently has been very powerful, not only for the bonds whose yields have been driven further into negative territory (and their prices thus driven higher) but also for

　　　　19

Exhibit 4.   Distribution of Negative-Yielding Bonds in the Barclays/Bloomberg Global Aggregate Bond Index by Geographical Distribution and Type

A. By Market/Region

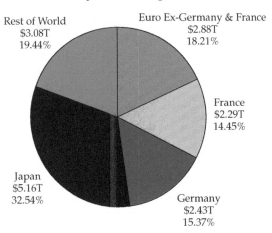

B. By Security Type

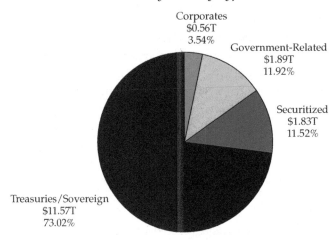

Note: All dollar amounts are shown in US dollar equivalents. Negative-yielding debt in the aggregate index was US$15.84 trillion as of 6 August 2020.
Source: Bianco Research, LLC. Used with permission.

the rest of the bond market (**Exhibit 6**). The rest of the bond market has had a total return since December 2018 almost three times higher than the total return on bonds with negative yields. Part of this is explained by the fact that when risk-free bonds have no yield, investors logically prefer some coupon

Exhibit 5.   US 10-Year Inflation-Linked Bond Yield, as of 7 August 2020

Source: Bianco Research, LLC. Used with permission

return and also some price return; the other part is that when there is no yield, the total return comes from an increase in prices. Because sovereign government bonds have a lower yield than corporate bonds, the effect of falling yields has been quite dramatic for bonds with higher coupons, which are composed of the corporate bond market and other "spread" products. Falling yields create a tidal demand for yield, which results in "all ships rising with the tide." As this monograph goes to production, bond markets have started to give back many of the gains as global economies recover and inflationary fears start to take center stage in investors' minds.

Why Are Interest Rates and Bond Yields Negative?

I propose two main hypotheses for the bond market trading at such negative yields. The first is the aggressive action of central banks due to (1) reducing deposit rates significantly below zero, (2) explicit purchase of long-term bonds ("quantitative easing"), and (3) expectation management ("forward guidance"), indicating that rates are likely to stay low for a very long time. The deposit

Exhibit 6.   Total Return of the Barclays/Bloomberg Global Aggregate Bond Index and the Negative-Yielding Bond Subindex, as of 6 August 2020

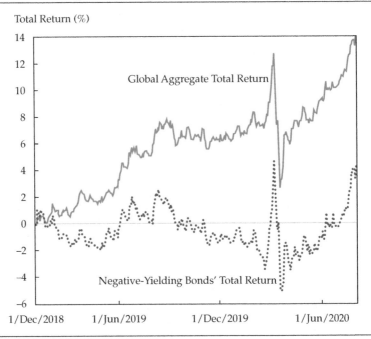

Source: Bianco Research, LLC. Used with permission.

rate set by the ECB has been progressively taken down below zero, and as of September 2020, it stands at −0.50%. The ECB has been buying and holding close to 30% of the outstanding debt in Europe, and the scarcity of outstanding debt could be a proximate cause for the rapid rise in prices and fall in yields. Although there has been talk of such sovereigns as Germany issuing very long-term bonds at negative yields, other than the anecdotal and relatively small issuance described in the previous paragraph, this issuance has been minimal so far. In short, demand has exceeded supply and has driven prices to a point where long-term bonds have traded at negative yields in the secondary market. We will return to central banks in a later chapter.

The second, competing hypothesis is that the market in aggregate is perhaps correctly forecasting future economic conditions and thus creating incentives to buy assets that hold their principal value even though doing so involves a high penalty, in terms of negative yields. This is because we can think of negative-yielding bonds as "options," where the lost capital is the option premium, and this premium guarantees repayment of most, though not all, of the investment at maturity. Fathoming in any detail what such an outcome might look like is difficult, but the fact that investors are willing to pay to lend suggests that this outcome, if priced correctly, is some sort of catastrophic one (e.g., deflation, default, a breakup of the European Union, or outright depression) that would certainly qualify as unprecedented in the historical context.

Another hypothesis is the possibility that a significant shift has occurred in time preferences due either to demographics or to what economists call Ricardian equivalence (i.e., people saving for future tax bills because they observe deficit spending in the present). If that is the case, investors are willing to receive less in the future than they are investing today. If this hypothesis is true, then one can argue that even though bonds have no return to speak of, they are not "return-free risky instruments" but rather "risk-free and return-free" deposit instruments when held for the very long term simply to guarantee future consumption.

In my view, the second hypothesis, though sound, is somewhat weak given that not only are sovereign bonds of such countries as Germany trading at negative yields but also are the bonds of such peripheral countries as Italy (below zero out to five years) and Greece (in the shortest maturity) (Hunter 2019). Furthermore, even some corporate bonds, such as those of Siemens (rated A), were issued and purchased at prices that imply negative yields if held to maturity (Davies 2019, Richter 2019). So, arguing that the protection of capital for future obligations is the primary driver of negative yields is difficult because corporates with weak credit ratings are not likely to be able to pay principal back in the catastrophic scenarios mentioned earlier unless the bonds are paid off by the sovereign. Some of these negatively yielding corporate bonds are indeed being purchased by central banks directly and indirectly as well.

To put this issue in context, what is interesting to note is the risk–reward trade-off of the aforementioned 30-year, zero-coupon bond. Because the bond's duration is 30 years, a 1% change in yield is enough for the bond to lose 30% of its value. The sensitivity, and perhaps the need for this interest rate sensitivity, is further illustrated by the demand of what has been called the "tulip king" or "Semper Augustus" of bonds with which we started this chapter: the 100-year maturity Austrian government bond (rating Aa1/AA+) maturing in June 2120, which very recently traded at a yield of 0.40% and which was issued at a yield of 0.88% in June 2020. To paraphrase the quote referencing tulips: Although few investors have had the opportunity to buy this bond, many have heard of it. The bond has a modified duration of more 70 years, which means that for a 1 bp move in yields, it loses almost two whole years of yield income. On the other hand, the bond has an enormous amount of positive convexity (63), again making our analogy with options stronger, which is desirable from the perspective of an investor who values this convexity. The positive convexity means that a further decline in yield will be tremendously profitable for the holder.

Clearly, holding either of the bonds just described is very risky from the perspective of potential price impact for any meaningful rise in yields, as long as the holding is shorter than the maturity period. This type of potential volatility is more common in such speculative investments as equities and commodities than in government bond markets, unless the bond satisfies some other portfolio construction need, such as risk mitigation or cash flow matching. Who buys these bonds in the face of significant market risk and for what reason is the topic addressed in the next chapter. There is no one "culprit" but a conglomeration of participants who have made the existence of such a market possible.

We will now switch gears to who buys negative-yielding bonds because clearly both these buyers and the bonds they buy exist, observing that this is not a fleeting situation but a market that is large enough for buyers and sellers to transact at prices that correspond to negative yields. But because we started with a reference to the Semper Augustus tulip, let us also note that part of the allure of owning a tulip with variegated colors was that it would eventually and unpredictably "break," often without much warning. The variegated colors were a consequence of a virus that had infected the tulip. The unpredictability in tulips, as in bonds, is undoubtedly appealing, as shown in the evolving culture of risk taking and speculation in financial markets.

Box 1: The "God Particle of Modern Finance"? What a 31-Year, Negative-Yielding, Zero-Coupon German Government Bond Means for Investors

---

The issuance on 21 August 2019 of a 31-year, zero-coupon bond at a negative yield was for me like finding the Higgs boson (aka the "God particle") was for a particle physicist in 2012. Although theory had predicted its existence a few decades earlier, the actual discovery was nonetheless stunning. Just as the discovery of the Higgs boson validated the otherwise hard-to-prove standard model of physics and invalidated other theories of the universe, the issuance and trading of a negative-yielding zero-coupon bond has validated, in my view, the theory that investment today is primarily about psychology, scarcity, need for safety, and, overwhelmingly, politics and much less about clean, economic arbitrage–free mathematical relationships, the time value of money, and the "no free lunch" axiom in which most finance professionals are trained.

Other zero-coupon bonds trade at negative yields in Germany (German government bonds are known by traders as "bunds"), over a half dozen of them. For example, the two-year maturity BKO ("Bundesschatzanweisungen") of 11 June 2021 trades at a yield of −0.86% and a price of €101.50. The DBR ("Bundesrepublik Deutschland) of 5 May 2024 maturity is a little less than five years to maturity and trades at a price of 104.18 today and a yield of −0.88%. The seven-year maturity zero trades at −0.82% and a price of 105.91. The 10-year maturity zero has a price of 106.66 and a yield of −0.65%. And of course, finally and most importantly, we have the 30+-year zero issued yesterday that trades at 103.35 today and a yield of −0.10%. Just by looking at the term structure of yields, one can roughly estimate the term structure of the price of insurance (for return *of* capital instead of return *on* capital) by subtracting 100 from the market price of the bond (e.g., 103.61 − 100 = 3.61). (All data here were taken from the Bloomberg terminal on 22 and 23 August 2019.)

The big deal is that bond investors assume that "anomalies" like negative yields are fleeting, and if that is the case, then the term structure of yields should reflect this. Depending on whom you speak with, roughly the five- to 10-year point is considered long enough for fundamental distortions in yields to be smoothed out. But 30+ years is a very long period and, until recently, beyond the reach of policymakers and governments; however, quantitative easing has changed all that. Our hero for this note is the 31-year-maturity German government zero-coupon bund issued on 21 August 2019, with a maturity date of 15 August 2050 and no call or put option provisions. It does not pay any interest until the maturity date. This is as simple and atomic as a bond ever gets, which is why understanding this "atomic" financial instrument is so important. This bond is basically equivalent to the "discount factor," with no need to engage in complex coupon stripping and discounting math. We can just read the discount factor from the price. The reason I call this bond the "God particle" is that it is the most fundamental building block of finance theory, because the risk-free discount factor is the fundamental building block of all financial math. Never in the history of bond trading has a 31-year, zero-coupon bond been issued at negative yields or above par in price. And until recently, it was considered an impossibility, at least in academic finance.

The price at issue was €103.61, and the redemption price will be exactly €100 [data are from Bloomberg, 21 August 2019]. Because the yield to

Description of 31-Year-Maturity, Zero-Coupon German Bond Issued at Negative Yield

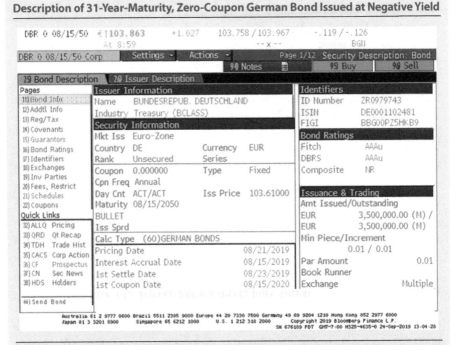

Note: In this description, the light text at center bottom says EUR BLN RETAINED FOR MARKET INTERVENTION. This bond has subsequently been re-issued such that the total outstanding amount in mid-2021 is close to €26 billion, out of which close to €10 billion is being held for market intervention.

Source: Used with permission of Bloomberg Finance L.P.

maturity is so close to zero, there is no present value computation to speak of, and all the bond math follows from one long division using pen and paper. Both in character and purity, this bund is breathtakingly "pure" in its valuation.

The consequences of the simplicity, however, are astounding. Just as a peek into the true nature of atomic physics shows the breathtaking simplicity and beauty of nature, a peek into the second grade math of a zero-coupon bond exposes where we appear to have come to in the world of finance. Because there is only one cash flow, the price of the bund is par (100) discounted back to today. We can simply say that the buyer of this bond is willing to pay 3.61% up front, or roughly 12 bps per year, to ensure that the nominal (i.e., not inflation adjusted) principal is returned. This bond has essentially no credit risk because Germany is widely noted to be one of the most responsible fiscal managers in the world. So, we can assume that the yield has negligible impurity from any other factor. The duration of a zero-coupon bond by definition is equal to the maturity of the bond.

Now, as we remember from our first bond math course, duration has two important definitions and interpretations. The Macaulay duration is the weighted average maturity of cash flows from a bond. Because there is only one cash flow at maturity, the Macaulay duration at issuance of this bund is 31 years. The intuition behind the Macaulay duration is that it is the "fulcrum" that balances the weight of the intermediate cash flows against the principal's return. So in this case, the fulcrum is at the maturity (i.e., both intuitively and mathematically, this bond's cash flows are akin to a very long lever, with the one and only pivot point at maturity). As Archimedes told us many years ago, "Give me a lever long enough and a fulcrum on which to place it, and I shall move the world"; here, the owner of the bond is taking on the risk of an incredible amount of potential return, positive or negative, for a very small change in yield.

This long-term zero at a price above par is very much like an Archimedean lever, and not too many of them are around, unless one uses derivatives or synthetic leverage. In other words, if you are an unlevered investor who can only buy bonds fully paid for in cash, you have no other choice than to buy this bond to obtain its price and yield trade-off, if that is what you desire.

Modified duration is the other important concept and is the sensitivity of the bond to yield changes—that is, the percentage price change for a small change in yield. For this German "bund," the modified duration is approximately 31 years; in other words, a 1% change in yield can change the price by approximately 31% of the bond's value.

The convexity of this bond, or the rate of change of the duration, is approximately 10 (i.e., for a large fall in yields, the bond's price will increase by a factor of the convexity times the square of the yield change, and for a large rise in yields, the bond's price will be cushioned by the convexity, leading to a significant amount of asymmetry). For a zero-coupon bond, the convexity is high anyway, increasing as the square of the maturity. For example, a cousin of this bond is the German bund maturing on 15 August 2029, which has a 10-year maturity. This 10-year zero has a convexity of "only" a tenth of that of the 30-year bond.

Combining the discussion of the previous two paragraphs, *this bond then provides a turbocharged call option on falling yields.* Not unlike Armageddon equity put options, a long-term zero-coupon bond is very much like an option on bond prices, thus the perceived demand from hedgers who need the convexity to hedge their long-term liabilities, which are also highly convex at these low interest rates. Bond math does not care (investors do) about negative and positive yields, so pushing yields further into negative territory exponentially increases the price of this bond. If an investor is buying this bond based on simply the price, which has no theoretical limit, then the more the need to diversify against equity market risk, the higher the price of this bond and the more rapid the rise in the price for the same decline in yield.

What about the perspective of the issuer of these bonds? Because no other unlevered instruments are in the market that can match the convexity of a zero-coupon bond, it is optimal for the issuer to issue while the supply of convexity is scarce. Meanwhile, demand from risk management needs is massive.

This is akin to the cycles in natural catastrophe reinsurance. The best time to sell insurance is when demand for insurance is high and supply is low. Of the almost €2 billion of the bund offered, less than €900 million was bought by buyers in the auction; the rest (almost €1.2 billion) was "retained for market intervention," (see previous Bloomberg screenshot) which presumably means that the bund will be fed out to the market if demand increases in the future. In other words, the public refused to pay as much money as the issuer wished for the privilege of lending money, so the buyer of last resort, the issuer or its affiliates, held the rest on its own books in reserve, maintaining the price.

Drawing further on the analogy with options, because the "time decay" of this option is so low per year, the cost of holding the bunds is negligible in the short run. Eventually, however, the bunds and the guaranteed loss on them will very likely be borne by European taxpayers. The most likely outcome is that indexed funds will be forced by their rules to buy these negative-yielding bunds. So far, this decade has seen record inflows into indexed bond funds, and, as will be discussed later, many of these indexed bond funds are passive buyers of negative-yielding global bonds. The flows are simply overwhelming the supply available, and if the issuer can keep the scarcity premium high enough, there will be willing buyers as long as a big reversal in bond market investment flows does not occur.

Note: The material here was excerpted from Bhansali (2019).

4. Who Buys Negative-Yielding Bonds, and Why?

> Lend not unto him that is mightier than thyself; for if thou lendest him, count it but lost.
>
> —*Ecclesiasticus 8:12, King James Version*

One of the most interesting phenomena in finance is investors' apparent willingness to part with something in exchange for nothing or (less dramatically) for something whose expected value is worth less than they paid for it. We know that financial insurance (e.g., the purchase of put options) is one example where investors are willing to pay a premium, which they typically expect to lose, in exchange for safety and risk transfer. In isolation, such a buy-and-hold long option strategy is a negative expected return investment. But this assertion is true only when we look at the put option in isolation; when we combine the value of a put option with other parts of a risky portfolio, owning put options can be justified by the put option's ability to truncate the "left tail" and add skew to the portfolio. That is, the put potentially tilts the distribution to one with more positive skew, less kurtosis, and less risk of permanent loss of capital (Bhansali 2014). Even without reference to the underlying portfolio, investors might prefer skewness for behavioral reasons. For instance, the demand for "lotteries" and call options has been well documented in the literature.

As discussed in the previous chapter, negative-yielding bonds exhibit many of the same option-like properties. When held to maturity, these bonds are guaranteed to be worth less than the value paid for them today. In other words, these bonds, which now make up almost 20% of the fixed-income markets, violate the centuries of basic understanding that a unit of riskless investment should nominally not be worth less in the future than it is today. The purpose of this chapter is to systematically evaluate the locally rational reasons a broad class of investors purchase negative-yielding bonds and to finally provide a bird's-eye view of the interrelationships between those investors' actions and the potential for global instability if the collective mindset toward the acceptable level of yields changes. This discussion will help shed light on why some market participants might be willing to lend to lose.

Even more importantly, the negative-yielding bond market is a unique laboratory in which the consequences of unprecedented easy monetary policy and the convergence between monetary and fiscal policy are being felt in real time, and in which the participants' actions, while locally rational, are linked by common risk factors that have the potential to be consequential for market risk management. If we believe that rational people invest money to achieve a positive rate of return, then, as discussed later, other factors necessarily have to account for why yields can be persistently negative for extended periods.

The simple and unnuanced answer to the question of who buys negative-yielding bonds is this: almost everyone! In broad terms, we can classify the buyers of negative-yielding bonds into three categories: (1) "forced" buyers, who have to buy them either for risk management reasons (e.g., pension liability hedgers, convexity hedgers) or because of their legal agreements (e.g., indexed exchange-traded funds); (2) discretionary buyers/speculators (e.g., currency-hedged investors or speculators looking for price appreciation, or carry traders); and (3) non-financially-motivated buyers (e.g., governments or their agencies, such as central banks).

Indexers and Passive Bond Exchange-Traded Funds

Bond fund management has seen two significant developments in the past decade. The first is a move toward standardization of bond indexes, and the second is the evolution of passive products, such as bond exchange-traded funds (ETFs) that have been built to mirror such market cap–weighted bond indexes.

Both these developments have been made possible by the increase in transparency, the reduction in transaction costs, and the increase in the size and quality of bond issuance and the data surrounding it. As a result of the fall in yields, passive bond funds that can be acquired at a cheap cost result in more net yield for investors and therefore improve their relative attractiveness in a world of low bond yields.

Because bonds have been well established as diversifiers against equity markets over the past three decades, many bond funds have found demand from portfolio managers of multi-asset portfolios.

A good example of a passive bond ETF is provided by the Vanguard Total International Bond ETF (BNDX). As required by law, the ETF publishes all its holdings daily for anyone to see. Digging into this ETF, we find it holding many of the negative-yielding bonds globally, as well as the Austrian "Semper Augustus" 100-year bond mentioned in the previous chapter. The advertised yield of this ETF was a little over 1% as of the end of the third quarter 2019, but a significant portion (almost 50 bps) of this yield comes from currency hedging, which we will discuss shortly in detail (Sources: Bloomberg, LongTail Alpha, LLC).

Indexers and passive bond ETFs are agents of their fund investors. They are required by their prospectus to purchase the bonds or to at least make an effort to replicate the bond holdings in their indexes. In the case of the BNDX, the index owns almost 11,000 securities, and to the degree that any new security is included in the index, BNDX will attempt to purchase it regardless of the price or yield. Because the index is market cap weighted, the lower the yield, the higher the price and the higher the allocation to that bond. Note that this is driven by the fact that the main perceived risk for an index ETF is tracking error, or the inability to replicate the return of the index; it is not the risk of poor absolute returns. Given this ETF's extremely low fee of only 8 bps a year, the agent's objective is to replicate the index, not attempt to add return through active management, whether by avoiding negative-yielding assets or through some other strategy.

While it might seem obvious that the passive bond funds are nondiscriminating buyers of bonds of all types and have therefore become the marginal price setters, including for bonds with negative yields, what is not so obvious is the sheer size and growth of these funds. BNDX has grown to approximately US$40 billion in assets (as of 2021) from almost nothing a decade ago, so even a small allocation to a bond in limited supply can have a substantial impact on that bond's price on the way up as well as on the way down when the bond is sold. If ETF holders aggressively redeem their fund holdings—as they attempted to do during the COVID-19 shock of March 2020 (before the Fed and other central banks stepped in)—they can create bond market illiquidity.

Liability Hedgers

The second large category of investors who are buyers of long-term bonds are pension funds and insurance companies. Their need for bonds is a function of the need both to diversify asset risk and to hedge the duration and convexity of their liabilities.

As interest rates fall, the present value of liabilities increases, and the longer the bond, the higher the need for convexity. To balance the asset–liability mix, these funds are thus required to acquire more interest duration. Because long-term fixed-income securities have a price-to-yield relationship that exhibits positive convexity, the more the yield drops, the more pensions need to hedge the duration of liabilities with larger and larger positions in longer-duration fixed-income instruments.

On the diversification front, note that a typical pension has a 0.60 equity beta, so we can also ask the question of what owning bonds or duration does for the pension fund portfolio's overall risk. For a 50% decline in the equity markets, this portfolio would be expected to lose approximately 30%. Assuming a duration of roughly 20 years on the fixed-income portfolio, a 200 bps decline in yields would return 40% if the portfolio had 100% allocation to long-duration fixed income. Although the market has levered fixed-income overlays for hedging, at a 40% allocation to fixed income, only 16 percentage points of the equity loss would be made up by the bond allocation. A 200 bps decline in yields would squarely put almost the entire US yield curve as of this writing into negative territory, and European yields would have to fall to deeply negative territory from current negative levels. Because of the needed response to falling yields, from a pure risk management perspective, longer-duration bonds are preferable for such hedgers, regardless of the bonds' current yield levels.

One could argue that rather than hedging with a negative-yielding security, an investor could simply store the future obligations in cash (i.e., under the proverbial "mattress"), pulling the cash out as needed to pay for the obligations. However, the reality is that this strategy would require large and costly storage vaults and involve the risk of theft and other frictions. Many countries have outlawed large-denomination bills to discourage such hoarding of cash, and as discussed in the introduction, many economists are advocating the same in the United States. So, as a practical matter, investing in the bond markets remains the only alternative available for the sheer size of such risk management-driven investments.

Systematic Traders

Systematic traders—such as risk parity strategies, volatility-targeting strategies, and trend followers or commodity-trading advisers—are large buyers of negative-yielding assets because of the historical and potential of future substantial price appreciation of even bonds with negative yields, as long as the price appreciation trend is rapid enough.

A simple way to understand this is by decomposing the total return of a bond instrument over any finite horizon into the expected return from changes in the shape of the yield curve and from the passage of time. We can think of the yield and roll-down of a bond as the expected return from the passage of time, and we can think of the price appreciation as emanating from the change in yield times the duration. If the total return is the sum of these two components, we can easily see why a negative yield for a bond, if accompanied by further price appreciation resulting from a rapid fall in yields, can still have positive *conditional* expected total return—conditioned on further yield declines—if held for a period less than the maturity of bond.

A good example of this dynamic was recently observed in the German bund market when the 10-year maturity bund yield dropped below the short-term deposit rate. With the deposit rate at −0.50% and the 10-year bund yielding −0.70%, buying and holding the bund to maturity is guaranteed to lose some of the principal, and for any finite holding horizon, the −0.20% of negative carry is also a return detractor. However, the duration of 10 years on the bond means that a 0.20% decline in yields would make up for the negative carry, as long as the price appreciated rapidly enough. Thus, the motivation for trend followers and other systematic investors is that price appreciation can make up for the losses from negative yield. The commonality between the ownership of negative-yielding bonds by many such systematic traders is that their decisions are based on prices and changes in prices rather than on yields to maturity. Many such systematic strategies have been adopted by large institutional investors as part of their diversification buckets. Again, this a reason for demand exceeding supply and perhaps driving and keeping yields in negative territory.

Speculators

Similarly, speculators who buy negative-yielding bonds are likely betting that the price of the negative-yielding bonds will rise over a short time horizon so that they can be sold to another buyer—perhaps a forced buyer or a central bank buyer—who will be willing to buy it at a higher price than what the speculator paid for it. Because most speculators do not intend to hold the bond to its maturity, we can think of this activity as driven primarily by short-term demand and supply.

This circumstance raises the question of whether a theoretical limit exists on how low or negative rates can become and whether we are indeed close to that limit. Because little historical evidence is available to support any claim of negative yield bounds, we have to speculate that the lower limit for yields is presumably a level at which an investor would simply choose to hold the money in cash, despite the risks and costs of holding large amounts of cash.

Arbitrageurs/Carry Traders

One extremely interesting participant in the negative-yielding bond markets is the cross-border investor, who can buy the negative-yielding bond and turn it into a positive-yielding bond via a short-term currency hedge.

As an example, consider a US investor looking to buy a 10-year German bund at a native (euro) yield of −0.50%. As of the end of third quarter 2019, the short-term interest rate in the money markets in the United States was approximately 2%, whereas the same in Europe was approximately −0.65%. Thus, the short-term interest rate differential was 2.65%. For a US buyer of German bunds, the total "yield" on the currency-hedged transaction was therefore 2.15%. The mechanics of this seemingly miraculous trade are revealed later in this chapter.

This "yield" on the hedged transaction is not a yield to maturity because for the term of the bond to realize the carry, the forward currency hedges must be rolled at the then-current rate spreads. Whether the carry trader is able to harvest the spread for that length of time or not thus depends critically on the rate differential persisting for the holding horizon of the bond.

There is an anecdote about three traders who decided to go into the business of trading sardines. The first trader bought a can of sardines for US$5. He sold the same can of sardines to the second trader for US$10, doubling his money. The second trader again doubled his money by selling the can of sardines to the third trader for US$20. The third trader, knowing very well that he was overpaying for the sardines, said to himself, "If the market for sardines crashed, at least I will be able to eat the sardines." The market did crash, and he opened the can to find that the sardines were rotten. He promptly went to the trader who had sold him the bad sardines and said, "These sardines are no good!" to which the second trader responded, "Of course they are no good for eating—they are trading sardines!"

Currency-hedged negative-yielding bonds are like these sardines. They do not provide a positive return in their own currency; they do so only when packaged with a currency hedge. These dressed-up bonds are being bought for trading, not for holding as investments.

What is the financial alchemy that in the short run can potentially turn negative yields into positive yields? To understand where I am going, the reader has only to know the meaning of the phrases "carry and roll-down" and "cross-currency hedging." Readers know that because of interest rate parity, a currency with a lower interest rate is likely to increase in value relative to other currencies in the future.

The implied forward exchange rates for any pair of currencies is determined by (1) the spot exchange rate, (2) the differential of the money market rates for that "tenor" (time to expiry of the security), and (3) the cross-currency basis swap, which essentially measures the demand and supply mismatch for the two currencies. For the purpose of this discussion, we do not need to understand the details of the basis swap. The only thing the reader must know is that if he buys a German bund at a negative yield of −0.35% and then hedges the currency risk by selling the euro currency forward to convert the proceeds over the hedge horizon into dollars, he is selling the forward

Exhibit 7. Example of Currency-Hedged Bond Yields as of 17 June 2019

FX-Hedged Yields	United States	Germany	France	Italy	United Kingdom	Japan	Australia	Canada
Dollar Investor	1.72%	2.08%	2.39%	3.56%	1.93%	2.28%	2.19%	1.86%
Euro Investor	(0.82)	(0.52)	(0.22)	0.92	(0.64)	(0.33)	(0.39)	(0.70)
Yen Investor	(0.70)	(0.40)	(0.10)	1.05	(0.52)	(0.21)	(0.27)	(0.58)

Source: LongTail Alpha, LLC.

exchange rate at a higher price than the spot exchange rate; so, the difference between the forward exchange rate and the spot exchange rate can be considered additional "yield" coming from the hedge.

In mid-2019, a very interesting situation occurred where most developed markets had a much lower unhedged yield than the US Treasury (except those of Italy), yet the hedged yield for every country's bonds was higher than the yield of the US 10-year Treasury (**Exhibit 7**). This is an example of what is called a "carry trade" in two ways.[3] Taking a long-term, low-yielding asset and using a derivatives contract turns a low yield temporarily into a high yield, and vice versa. The lower policy rates in foreign countries resulted in a carry benefit in the "internal" market as well as in the "external" market.

For example, in Europe, very negative short-term yields (−0.69%) result in positive carry, even for a 10-year bund at −0.35% for internal European buyers, such as indexers or euroland banks. This is because if one buys a bond at −0.35% with a fixed yield curve shape, the bond rolls down toward the more negative shorter-term yield, which results in positive total return. Indeed, the increasing TARGET2 (Trans-European Automated Real-Time Gross Settlement Express Transfer System 2) deficits of Italy and others (TARGET2 is operated by the Eurosystem) are a symptom of the fact that money was recycled from Italy and other peripheral countries back into German bunds, presumably because despite negative yields, the carry and safety of being in German bunds was worth the risks to Italian holders of euros and Italian bonds because Germany is much more creditworthy than Italy (**Exhibit 8**).

This state of affairs has a classic life cycle and is related to other forms of carry trades. The currency carry trade is also deeply related to the volatility in currencies and other asset classes (Bhansali 2007). The fact that currency volatility has remained incredibly low over the past decade has so far mitigated forced unwinds of leverage in this carry strategy.

---

[3]In a carry trade, an investor implicitly or explicitly borrows money in one market at a lower interest cost and invests it for potentially higher interest income in another market.

Exhibit 8. Germany and Italy TARGET2 Balances, as of March 2019

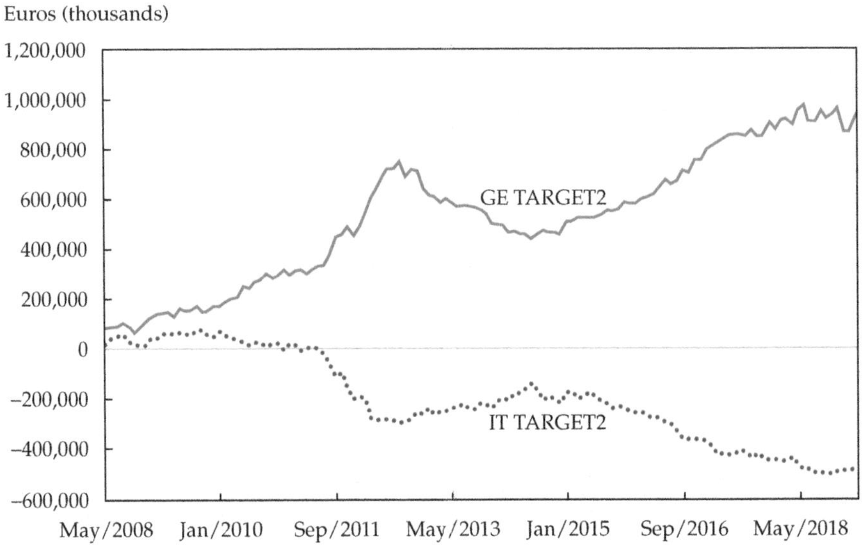

Euros (thousands)

Source: LongTail Alpha, LLC.

Whenever a type of financial alchemy (1) turns high into low and low into high, (2) uses a "yield curve" or "cross-currency" mismatch, (3) is exposed to shocks to volatility, (4) uses a derivatives contract that needs to be rolled periodically, and (5) depends on central bank policy for its benefits to continue, one should become cautious. In the case of the global government bond markets, the currency hedging tail can wag the bond dog. Yield curve inversions within one currency's bond markets can cause mayhem to bond markets by upsetting the "carry" arbitrage between maturities. Similarly, a sudden collapse in cross-currency interest rate differentials and upward shocks to currency volatility or to forward exchange rates between two different currencies can create chaos in currency markets. Interestingly, this "arbitrage" has become somewhat institutionalized. The US$1.5 trillion Government Pension Investment Fund (GPIF) of Japan, one of the largest pension investors in the world, announced in 2019 that it would reclassify currency-hedged foreign bonds as domestic Japanese bonds (Appell 2019).

Repo Use

Levered financial institutions use "repos" or repurchase agreements for financing their asset holdings. A repo is a transaction in which a security can be lent for a fixed interest rate for a fixed amount of time. Depending on the security's perceived riskiness, the lender of cash might apply a "haircut" to the security's market value to determine how much cash to lend in exchange. For example, a risky sovereign bond, such as one from Greece, might require a much larger haircut, while a high-credit-quality bond, such as a German bund, might have almost no haircut. Because financial markets operate by recycling such collateral, also known as rehypothecation, the lower the haircut, the more times the collateral can be reused in funding transactions.

A liquid, safe bond might therefore carry a much lower yield than a risky bond because it is higher-quality collateral, and as such, it can be used many times over. German bunds, even with their negative yields, are one of the securities that provide a safety and scarcity premium, and their value as collateral in repo operations is so high that investors might be willing to forgo yield to be able to use them as collateral for financing. (For more discussion on this topic, see Minenna, Boi, and Verzella 2016 and Arrata, Nguyen, Rahmouni-Rousseau, and Vari 2018.)

Central Banks

In the aftermath of the global financial crisis and COVID-19, the balance sheet of the four largest central banks of the world has mushroomed to almost US$25 trillion (**Exhibit 9** and **Exhibit 10**). As part of its debt buybacks, the ECB has been a large buyer of negative-yielding bonds. For instance, the 31-year German zero-coupon bond issued in September 2019 and discussed in the previous chapter was issued in a total size of €3.5 billion, but €1.176 billion was "retained for market intervention." In other words, not only are central banks buying these bonds in the open market, but they also are purchasing them in the primary issuance at negative yields, in many cases reducing the total net supply of the bonds.

Because ascribing a financial profit motive to a central bank is difficult, I will classify these banks as nonfinancial buyers whose purchases are designed to achieve economic and geopolitical objectives other than financial profits. In the case of the ECB, one such objective is to maintain the integrity of the euro currency and the monetary union of the eurozone countries that currently have little, if any, fiscal integration.

In 2020, the European system moved one step closer to fiscal integration as "common bonds" were approved and issued (Davies 2021). For example, the zero-coupon EU common bond maturing in July of 2035 was issued at €101.50 on 24 November 2020 and will pay no coupons until maturity (European Union SURE bond). The final redemption value will be €100,

Exhibit 9. Total Assets of the Four Largest Central Banks: Fed, ECB, BOJ, and PBOC

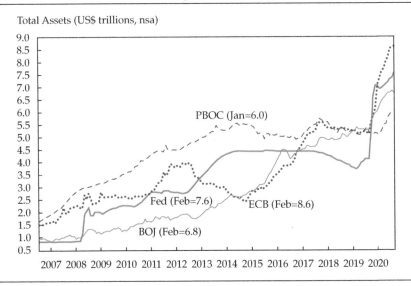

Total Assets (US$ trillions, nsa)

Note: BOJ = Bank of Japan; PBOC = People's Bank of China.
Source: Yardeni Research.

Exhibit 10. Combined Total Assets of the Four Largest Central Banks: Fed, ECB, BOJ, and PBOC

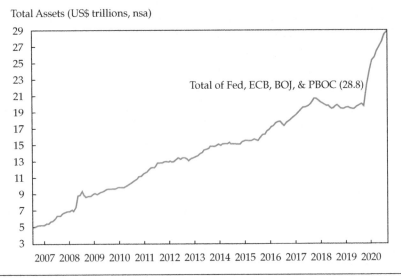

Total Assets (US$ trillions, nsa)

Note: BOJ = Bank of Japan; PBOC = People's Bank of China.
Source: Yardeni Research.

which translates into a yield of −0.105%. The money received was disbursed to the EU nations under the SURE (Support to mitigate Unemployment Risks in an Emergency) program. The €8.5 billion bonds were issued at a yield roughly 25 bps higher than that of the German bund of roughly the same maturity to induce buyers to earn a spread over the German bunds (but buyers would still be paying for the privilege of holding the bonds and lending money).

The argument can again be made that the action of central banks and their impact on bonds is obvious because they have made engineering low rates to stimulate demand and consumer price inflation via the traditional channels part of their policy. However, some agree that quantitative easing, especially in Europe and Japan, has not resulted in the desired economic outcomes or a rise in consumer price inflation to target levels. The next logical step in the experimentation was "going direct" or what has been called "helicopter money," that is, transfers directly to the public (Bartsch, Boivin, Fischer, and Hildebrand 2019), which began with various fiscal stimulus programs around the globe in 2020 during the COVID-19 crisis. This action brought monetary and fiscal policy closer together and potentially makes negative yields a more permanent fixture of financial markets.

Other Factors

Another possibility is that the current negative-yield environment is not due just to the action of the participants mentioned earlier but also to other possibilities, such as negative time preference. This hypothesis would argue that investors are more worried about the return of their capital than about the return on their capital, and to ensure this outcome, they are willing to part with some of their principal. An increasing cohort of retirees looking to save for retirement could result in exactly this type of environment. Another possibility is that some of the holders of negative-yielding assets are "underground" holders of cash, primarily in the US dollar and the euro. As reported by Rogoff (2020), recent estimates suggest that roughly one-half of the currency printed by the Fed and the ECB ends up overseas. For safekeeping, owners of this cash have a trade-off to make. They could potentially store the cash "under a mattress," which, depending on the risk of confiscation or seizure, might be a more costly alternative than just putting the money in a bank that would effectively charge a price to do so. Given the larger size of the underground economy, the potential scale of tax avoidance in Europe could be twice that in the United States (Rogoff 2020), which is another possible reason that rates are more persistently negative in Europe.

Pushing this reasoning further via the example used earlier in this monograph (Mankiw 2009), assume that there was a random chance, say 10%, that an illegal hoarder of cash could be discovered and all his cash subsequently confiscated by authorities. The hoarder would rationally be willing to deposit his cash in a bank account with a small negative yield because the expected value in that case would still be higher than if he lost everything by having his illegal activities discovered.

Finally, the distinct possibility exists that at least in Europe, negative yields are a way for the holder of, say, German bunds to be compensated for a breakup in the euro. If after the hypothetical breakup the new euro were a "German euro," then today, an owner of this euro should be willing to take a much lower yield in exchange for the currency's potentially much higher real value in the future.

Clearly, this chapter highlights that investors might want to buy negative-yielding bonds for a host of reasons. The most important participants are the central banks, to whom we turn next in some detail.

5. The Central Role of Central Banks

> From the point of view of sequences of government IOUs called bonds and money, institutional arrangements that delegate decisions about bonds and money to people who work in different agencies are details. Central bank independence is a convention or a fiction.
>
> —*Marco Bassetto and Thomas Sargent, "Shotgun Wedding: Fiscal and Monetary Policy"*

No discussion of the bond markets today can ignore the key role of central banks. Central banks came into existence in the 17th century (1694) with the establishment of the Bank of England as a way for the government to procure a war loan for £1.2 million at a rate of 8%, secured by tonnage duties. In addition, this "Governor and Company of the Bank of England" would have the right to trade in bullion and bills of exchange, engage in banking business, and issue bank notes up to an amount equal to its capital funds. Its privileges would cease when the principal of the loan was repaid, but not before 1706; the bank's charter has repeatedly been renewed, and it survives to this date as the central bank of the United Kingdom (Homer and Sylla 2005).

The US Fed was organized in 1913 after a number of market crises and the failure of a few attempts at creating a bank of banks. The Fed charter permitted government officials to influence interest rates by methods that had long been used in Europe and created a monopoly on currency issuance. According to historians of the Fed, its influence has served to lower interest rates below what they would otherwise have been in periods of both falling and rising interest rates. In addition, according to Homer and Sylla (2005),

> towards the turn of the twentieth century, the early concept of permanent annuity lost most of its appeal and investors became maturity conscious; investors, in other words, evinced a livelier desire to secure the payment of their principal and less concern for an assured income. (p. 497)

This maturity dependence, and the willingness to receive no or even negative interest, has resulted in the evolution of both the yield curve and its most recent incarnation, the negative yield curve, which has become a potent weapon of monetary strategy in Europe and Japan so far. When rates and yields are negative, monetary and fiscal policy become coupled ever more tightly because the fiscal authority (e.g., the government) issues bonds at negative yields while the monetary authority prints money to buy these bonds at negative yields, thus transferring future value into the present via an explicit transfer of cash.

If fiscal and monetary policy are now converging as a result of a global phenomenon of reliance on the government (one might ask why, and this author has no definitive explanations), then we could observe yield curves in all countries going negative. Can the United States, with the US dollar's role as the reserve currency of the world and the "exorbitant privilege" of being able to flood the markets with dollars without the currency proportionately losing value, be far behind in going negative? For now, the US Federal Reserve has declined to take interest rates negative, instead stating that it has other mechanisms to achieve the same objectives. Given that the Fed is the most powerful central bank in the world, we have to accept this statement at face value because, despite its various historical trials and tribulations, the Fed has had more experience than any other central bank in managing the spending needs of a central government versus the considerations of a fiscal union of its component states.

Central banks have traditionally controlled the short-term rate and ultimately credit via fractional reserve banking. In such a system, the central bank can change the reserve requirements at a commercial bank or indirectly allow for the quantity of money at the commercial banks to change based on its policy. Because the banks can loan some multiple of the reserve, the amount of liquidity and interest rates in the system change with the central bank's policy through a multiplicative process. In the United States, the Fed controls the short maturity federal funds rate and the discount rate. Once short-term rates are set, in principle, long-term rates are, among other things, a function of the path of these short-term rates. Long-term rates are essentially the average of the short-term rates that are expected to occur in the future plus a possible risk or horizon premium for having to wait for one's money. Any signal about asymmetric policy in the future is transmitted through the yield curve by the act of market participants interpreting the signal (Bhansali, Dorsten, and Wise 2009). We will ignore the horizon premium for the current discussion.

In the United States, the general consensus, despite never being explicitly acknowledged by the Fed, is that its policy rule roughly targets a short-term rate that balances inflation and unemployment, which are the two official inputs to the legal dual mandate of the Fed. This rule is called the Taylor rule: The Fed raises nominal short-term interest rates (tightening policy) if inflation is higher than a target inflation rate (called π^*) or if unemployment falls below a certain unemployment rate, called the NAIRU (non-accelerating inflation rate of unemployment),[4] labeled u^*. An example of a Taylor rule is a simple linear reaction function for the nominal short-rate target, r_N:

$$r_N = r^* + \pi + [\alpha \times (\pi - \pi^*)] + [\beta \times F \times (u^* - u)].$$

Formally, this simple-looking linear regression rule can be derived as the solution to an economic problem that reduces the total variability or volatility in unemployment and inflation, or the minimization of a quadratic loss function of unemployment and inflation. As of late 2020, with repeated misses in meeting the inflation target, the Fed adopted an enhancement of this rule termed the FAIT (flexible average inflation targeting), where the Fed would not target realized inflation at a point in time but rather use an average of realized inflation over an undefined period. On balance, market participants have interpreted this enhancement as meaning that the Fed will tolerate higher, asymmetric increases in inflation as opposed to a sharp decrease in inflation toward the zero bound in nominal interest rates, because the latter could result in a liquidity trap, such as the one that has occurred in Japan over the past two decades.

As of June 2020, and following the COVID-19 economic shock, the explicit value of the parameters in this Taylor rule would have been as follows (see **Exhibit 11**):

$$-5.77 = 2 + 1.02 + [0.50 \times (1.02 - 2.00)] + [0.50 \times 2.00 \times (5.00 - 13.30)].$$

A naive application of this rule shows that in periods of financial stress, such as the ones that occurred during the global financial crisis and again in early 2020, the nominal federal funds rate would have to be deeply negative. Because long-term bond yields are formed by the expectation for short-term rates in the future, by a simple application of continuous compounding of the short-term rate, we can see that if central banks promise low or negative rates into the indefinite future—as they have done via the mechanism of "forward guidance" or expectations management—then long-term yields will also fall. Because prices of bonds are inversely proportional to yields, lower bond yields imply higher bond prices, and the lower the yields, the higher the rate of change in bond returns. The credibility of the central bank plays a critical role

---

[4]This version of the Taylor rule uses the standard definition of r^* for the unobserved but much debated neutral real rate of interest, π and π^* for the current rate of core Personal Consumption Expenditures (PCE) price index inflation (in the United States) and target PCE inflation of 2%, and Okun's law, which relates the unemployment rate u, the NAIRU u^*, to potential and actual economic growth with a factor of two.

Exhibit 11. The Naive Taylor Rule Projected a Federal Funds Rate of Almost –6% Given That Unemployment in the United States Spiked to Almost 13% in the Aftermath of the COVID-19 Crisis

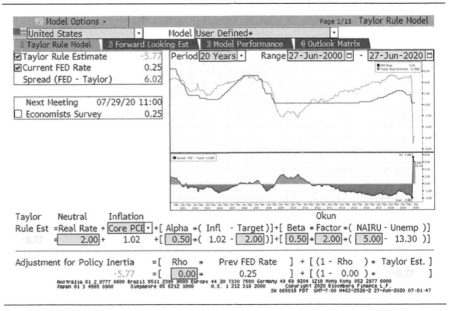

Source: Used with permission of Bloomberg Finance L.P.

in the evolution of the yield curve, especially when the market can translate the policy function into rules.

Other global central banks have their own mandates and rules to achieve these mandates. For instance, the ECB has a single mandate, which is to target price stability as per the Maastricht Treaty. Central bankers are held accountable, whether implicitly or explicitly, for meeting certain numerical targets on a specific metric, such as 2% inflation. This quantitative approach to managing the economy can have important unintended consequences for both asset prices and the economy.

Central banks recently have been forced to deal with a set of conditions where their primary tool for implementing monetary policy, the level of interest rates, has essentially run out of potency. The "zero bound" of nominal interest rates means that central banks cannot stimulate the economy by conventional means because the "rules" require rates to be negative, but there is a practical limit to how negative interest rates can become.

To deal with the problem of the inability of traditional tools in addressing the need for negative nominal interest rates, many new monetary and fiscal tools have been invented. The interaction of monetary and fiscal policy near the zero bound has been justified as a necessity to ensure a quick escape from recessions (see Hoffman, Lombardi, Mojon, and Orphanides 2020). First, central banks have used quantitative easing, which is essentially a tool to print cash and purchase longer-term bonds, thereby exchanging short-term debt (i.e., cash) for longer-term debt. The idea here is that by lowering long-term interest rates, one can engineer expectations of easy future financial conditions. As discussed previously, the four major central banks (Fed, ECB, Bank of Japan, and People's Bank of China) have collectively bought close to US$25 trillion of bonds using the cash they created.

Second, the banks have used "forward guidance," which essentially promises the market that although a central bank cannot engineer growth and inflation today, it is committing to raising inflation in the future by keeping monetary policy accommodative for longer.

Third, by signaling a higher inflation target, and asymmetry in terms of tolerating higher inflation, central banks expect that even with lower nominal rates, the real interest rate (given that Real interest rate = Nominal interest rate − Inflation rate) will be driven more negative, thus stimulating the economy that is theoretically driven by real interest rates.

Finally, by taking interest rates into negative territory, central banks hope that money will be taken out of deposit accounts and invested in the real economy.

Because inflation is such an important metric in the current rhetoric of all central banks, a comment about metrics is appropriate. Campbell's Law (written in the context of research methodologies more generally than Goodhart's Law) states, "The more any quantitative social indicator is used for social decision-making, the more subject it will be to corruption pressures and the more apt it will be to distort and corrupt the social processes it is intended to monitor" (Campbell 1979). Inflation can be measured, but it is only one input into economic and welfare decisions, and too much energy is possibly being spent on measuring something that might not be relevant in the long run for economic welfare. In other words, according to a famous quote that is attributed to Einstein, "Not everything that can be counted is worth counting, and not everything that is worth counting can be counted."

One school of thought is that by fixating on one metric, central banks might be creating collateral risks (i.e., an asset price bubble). Negative rates could result in high asset prices, which make markets less attractive and more vulnerable to crashes; when the crashes happen, more central bank action is required, starting another cycle of leveraging and deleveraging. The formal policy rules have the goal of raising inflation and stimulating growth. However, after almost two decades of experimentation, especially in Japan, with both conventional and unconventional tools, inflation has not convincingly and consistently risen to the central banks' target levels.

Most central banks today ignore asset prices as a direct input in the computation of inflation metrics. Almost 50 years ago, Alchian and Klein (1973) argued that a good measure of inflation should include asset prices. The theoretical argument is that conventional measures of inflation yield an incomplete picture of inflation conditions because consumers care about the changes not only in the prices of the goods they currently buy but also in the prices of goods they are likely to buy in the future. In other words, consumers do not make just annual cost of living adjustments based on current inflation but estimate a lifetime cost of living based on current and expected future income and expected expenses.

A simplified form for the Alchian and Klein measure of inflation π_{AK} is $\pi_{AK} = \alpha \pi_C + (1 - \alpha)\pi_{AP}$, where π_C is conventional (consumer price) inflation and π_{AP} is asset price inflation. Empirical analysis has been mixed on whether asset price inflation causes consumer price inflation and whether including it in the inflation calculation results in prospectively better economic decisions. While housing inflation does show some impact on consumer price inflation—presumably because housing is an element of the consumer price calculation—stock market inflation has a much weaker impact on consumer inflation. However, a sharp sell-off in equity prices has been observed to have a negative impact on spending due to an increase in risk aversion and thus a negative effect on inflation in the short run. This leads to the natural conclusion that central banks implicitly do target asset prices in setting policy via the rationale that asset prices are an essential ingredient of "financial stability," which can, indeed, affect growth and inflation.

The Alchian–Klein measure is much more volatile than the consumer price inflation series for weights of $\alpha \neq 1$ because of high equity market volatility. Reacting to a very volatile series to make policy rules that act only with lags would certainly be a risky proposition from the perspective of managing the economy (**Exhibit 12**). However, most market participants would likely agree that actual monetary policy does respond to volatility that is primarily driven by asset prices. Thus, a strong argument can be made that asset prices need to be included explicitly in some form in the mandate for central banks so that policy reaction functions are more transparent.

Exhibit 12. Consumer Price Inflation and Alchian–Klein Measure of Inflation

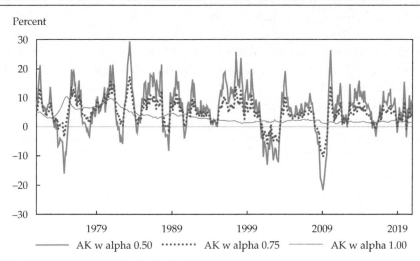

Percent

——— AK w alpha 0.50   ·········· AK w alpha 0.75   ——— AK w alpha 1.00

Note: This exhibit shows the consumer inflation rate, as measured by the PCE price index (the thin blue line), and an adjusted inflation rate using the Alchian–Klein (AK) approach of weighting inflation with asset price growth rates.
Source: LongTail Alpha, LLC.

Monetary policymaking is an art, even though the 20th century infatuation with machines and the physical world might have convinced many that it can be transformed into engineering—that is, distilled down to repeatable rules of cause and effect. The history of policymaking is full of mistakes that were not corrected until many years later with the benefit of hindsight, and in this author's view, current monetary policy principles should be taken with lots of caveats as well. Central banks are populated by economists who have gone to similar graduate schools and who have studied the same academic papers and books. Many central bank leaders have in fact had the same PhD advisors. Anecdotally, both Ben Bernanke (former US Fed chair) and Mario Draghi (former ECB president) had Stanley Fischer on their doctoral committees and espoused the same type of theories.[5] As agents of the government, central bankers undoubtedly mean well, but there is increasing skepticism of the central banking philosophy of dealing with all problems as though they were problems of liquidity ("to a hammer, everything looks like a nail"). Errors can be made and defended because economic forecasting and regime-shift identification are incredibly difficult. "During the crisis in

---

[5]David Harrison, "How Stan Fischer Became a Global Central Banking Giant," *Wall Street Journal* (6 September 2017).

the 1930s, as the US and much of the world economy entered a depression, the Federal Reserve met the crisis in traditional fashion by raising interest rates. As in 1920–21, there was an official policy of deflation in the midst of depression" (Homer and Sylla 2005 p. 523). Milton Friedman, and later, Ben Bernanke, said that this error caused an ordinary depression to turn into the Great Depression.

Sociologists have written extensively on the perils of groupthink and the establishment of paradigms that change only when facts show that strongly held assumptions are clearly wrong. Until then, one should keep in mind this quip of John Kenneth Galbraith's (himself an economist): "Economists are economical, among other things, of ideas; most make those of their graduate days do for a lifetime." Or, observing some recent actions of the ECB's changing objective but relatively unchanged actions, the following quote from George Santayana might apply, in some people's opinion: "Fanaticism consists in redoubling your efforts when you have forgotten your aim."

With these warnings in mind, let us take a deeper look into the economic philosophy of the ECB, which has the arguably impossible task of setting monetary policy for a union of heterogeneous European countries in the absence of a fiscal union. The reason to choose the ECB for our deep dive is that Europe has had the most persistent negative interest rates, it has had them for a considerable amount of time, and the rates affect a considerable amount of bond capital. When we turn to the next chapter on asset pricing, these facts, combined with the global flow of capital, will make the importance of ECB policy extremely relevant to our discussion.

A Deeper Look at the ECB Monetary Policy

The ECB is the central bank for the nations of the eurozone, which is a very large subset of the European Union and is directly responsible for setting the interest rates and influencing bond yields, as shown in **Exhibit 13**. To "maintain price stability" is the primary objective of the Eurosystem and of the single monetary policy for which it is responsible. This is laid down in the Treaty on the Functioning of the European Union, Article 127 (1). The treaty establishes a clear hierarchy of objectives for the Eurosystem. "The Treaty makes clear that ensuring price stability is the most important contribution that monetary policy can make to achieve a favourable economic environment and a high level of employment."[6]

---

[6]"Objective of Monetary Policy," ECB website, https://www.ecb.europa.eu/mopo/intro/objective/html/index.en.html.

Exhibit 13.   ECB Deposit Rates and Long-Term German Bund Yields

Sources: Bloomberg, LongTail Alpha, LLC.

Price stability is currently defined by a unique metric (though the policy is under review at the time of this writing) as a "'year-on-year increase in the Harmonised Index of Consumer Prices (HICP) for the euro area of below 2%.' The Governing Council clarified in 2003 that in the pursuit of price stability it aims to maintain inflation rates below, but close to, 2% over the medium term."[7]

The term "harmonized" denotes the fact that all the countries in the eurozone follow the same methodology. This ensures that data for one country can be compared with data for another. The benefits, according to the ECB, of putting a figure on price stability is that it "makes the monetary policy more transparent; provides a clear and measurable yardstick against which the European citizens can hold the ECB accountable; provides guidance to the public for forming expectations of future price developments."[8]

---

[7]"The Definition of Price Stability," ECB website, https://www.ecb.europa.eu/mopo/strategy/pricestab/html/index.en.html.
[8]Ibid.

Because the central bank is the "monopoly supplier" of the monetary base, it can "set conditions at which banks borrow from the central bank. Therefore it can also influence the conditions at which banks trade with each other in the money market." The ECB further goes on to explain that this hypothesis is based on the "long-run neutrality of money" and that "it is widely agreed that in the long run . . . a change in the quantity of money in the economy will be reflected in a change in the general level of prices."[9]

Critics of this inflation-target-based approach have responded in two ways: First, the long run can be really long ("in the long run, we are all dead"), so this hypothesis is impossible to test. Second, as two Nobel prize–winning economists (George Akerlof and Robert Shiller) have argued, this is an inaccurate description of the world and depends on the assumption that individuals do not suffer from money illusion (Akerlof and Shiller 2009). Money illusion, in simplest terms, is the bias to think of money in nominal, rather than real, terms, mistaking the face value of money for its purchasing power.

The theory underlying the grand monetary experiment is summarized in the Friedmanian interpretation by the ECB that "ultimately, inflation is a monetary phenomenon. Prolonged periods of high inflation are typically associated with high monetary growth. While other factors (such as variations in aggregate demand, technological changes or commodity price shocks) can influence price developments over shorter horizons, over time their effects can be offset by a change in monetary policy."[10]

In **Box 2**, I reproduce in full the "Transmission Mechanism of Monetary Policy," a publication on the ECB's website that lays out the mechanics of how monetary policy *should* transmit through the economy. As the reader can observe, the simplified, mechanical description seems to suggest a deep belief in a causal "flowchart," with deterministic pathways and causes leading to effects. From this viewpoint, any failure to generate outcomes means that either one of the connectors in the flow diagrams is not operating efficiently or perhaps the mechanical depiction is too simplistic and inaccurate. The fictional Captain Jack Sparrow of the *Pirates of the Caribbean* films would likely say: "The problem is not the problem. The problem is your attitude about the problem."

---

[9]"Scope of Monetary Policy," ECB website, https://www.ecb.europa.eu/mopo/intro/role/html/index.en.html.

[10]Ibid.

Box 2:   Transmission Mechanism of Monetary Policy
(Monetary Policy of the ECB, 2020)

This is the process through which monetary policy decisions affect the economy in general and the price level in particular. The transmission mechanism is characterised by long, variable and uncertain time lags. Thus it is difficult to predict the precise effect of monetary policy actions on the economy and price level.

The chart provides a schematic illustration of the main transmission channels of monetary policy decisions.

ECB's Model of How Credit Flows in the Economy

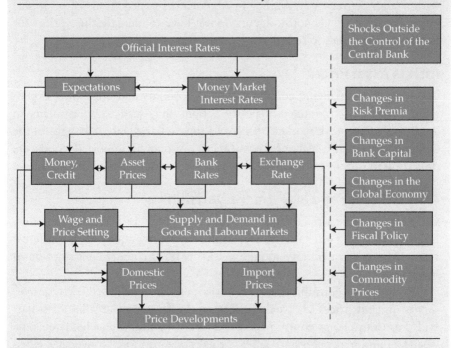

Change in Official Interest Rates

The central bank provides funds to the banking system and charges interest. Given its monopoly power over the issuing of money, the central bank can fully determine this interest rate.

Affects Banks and Money-Market Interest Rates

The change in the official interest rates affects directly money-market interest rates and, indirectly, lending and deposit rates, which are set by banks to their customers.

Affects Expectations

Expectations of future official interest-rate changes affect medium and long-term interest rates. In particular, longer-term interest rates depend in part on market expectations about the future course of short-term rates.

Monetary policy can also guide economic agents' expectations of future inflation and thus influence price developments. A central bank with a high degree of credibility firmly anchors expectations of price stability. In this case, economic agents do not have to increase their prices for fear of higher inflation or reduce them for fear of deflation.

Affects Asset Prices

The impact on financing conditions in the economy and on market expectations triggered by monetary policy actions may lead to adjustments in asset prices (e.g. stock market prices) and the exchange rate. Changes in the exchange rate can affect inflation directly, insofar as imported goods are directly used in consumption, but they may also work through other channels.

Affects Saving and Investment Decisions

Changes in interest rates affect saving and investment decisions of households and firms. For example, everything else being equal, higher interest rates make it less attractive to take out loans for financing consumption or investment.

In addition, consumption and investment are also affected by movements in asset prices via wealth effects and effects on the value of collateral. For example, as equity prices rise, share-owning households become wealthier and may choose to increase their consumption. Conversely, when equity prices fall, households may reduce consumption.

Asset prices can also have impact on aggregate demand via the value of collateral that allows borrowers to get more loans and/or to reduce the risk premia demanded by lenders/banks.

Affects the Supply of Credit

For example, higher interest rates increase the risk of borrowers being unable to pay back their loans. Banks may cut back on the amount of funds they lend to households and firms. This may also reduce the consumption and investment by households and firms respectively.

Leads to Changes in Aggregate Demand and Prices

Changes in consumption and investment will change the level of domestic demand for goods and services relative to domestic supply. When demand exceeds supply, upward price pressure is likely to occur. In addition, changes in aggregate demand may translate into tighter or looser conditions in labour and intermediate product markets. This in turn can affect price and wage-setting in the respective market.

Affects the Supply of Bank Loans

Changes in policy rates can affect banks' marginal cost for obtaining external finance differently, depending on the level of a bank's own resources, or bank capital. This channel is particularly relevant in bad times such as a financial crisis, when capital is scarcer and banks find it more difficult to raise capital.

In addition to the traditional bank lending channel, which focuses on the quantity of loans supplied, a risk-taking channel may exist when banks' incentive to bear risk related to the provision of loans is affected. The risk-taking channel is thought to operate mainly via two mechanisms. First, low interest rates boost asset and collateral values. This, in conjunction with the belief that the increase in asset values is sustainable, leads both borrowers and banks to accept higher risks. Second, low interest rates make riskier assets more attractive, as agents search for higher yields. In the case of banks, these two effects usually translate into a softening of credit standards, which can lead to an excessive increase in loan supply.

Note: The material here was reproduced from https://www.ecb.europa.eu/mopo/html/index.en.html. "Transmission Mechanism of Monetary Policy," ECB website, www.ecb.europa.eu/mopo/intro/transmission/html/index.en.html.

The first thing to note from Box 2 is that the "transmission mechanism is characterised by long, variable and uncertain time lags. Thus it is difficult to predict the precise effect of monetary policy actions on the economy and price level." The channels by which monetary policy is expected to act are through lower short-term interest rates, lower long-term interest rates, asset prices, increased availability of loans, expectations, and other factors. Testing in any finite period whether or not the theory is working in practice is therefore impossible. Given the ECB's strong belief that time lags can be long, variable, and uncertain, the policy has been to increase the stimulus (e.g., negative interest rates, long-term bond purchases to the tune of €40 billion a month, expectations management, and long-term loans at favorable rates). Asset prices have indeed responded globally as the tsunami of cheap cash has flooded the system, both in Europe and internationally.

While inflation as of this writing has been much lower than the 2% target, long-term projections suggest that the ECB staff does not believe that the rate of change in the HICP, the primary target of the policy, will rise to that level anytime soon. The projection of the "Survey of Professional Forecasters Q1 2020" is 1.2% for 2020, 1.4% for 2021, and 1.5% for 2022; longer-term expectations are at 1.7% (European Central Bank 2020).

Many euro area banks have to pay to deposit funds at the central bank, though many banks are able to access long-term "loans" at negative interest rates, as long as they make a certain amount of loans to the public. Recently, recognizing this problem, the ECB has started to create incentives to give banks money using preferential borrowing rates that are even more negative than the deposit rate (subtracting a more negative number from a less negative number results in a positive number!).

We can summarize the situation as follows:

- The ECB believes that its mandate is to achieve a numerical inflation target.

- To achieve its target, the ECB has various traditional and unconventional tools that it is willing and able to use.

- The forecast for the targets determines the scope and extent of the tools, which are essentially unlimited.

- The indirect effects on asset prices are, for the moment, less important than the mandate.

As described in a publication that set the stage for ever more negative rates on 12 June 2014 (European Central Bank 2014), the initial step to move the deposit rate into negative territory (of −0.10%) was somewhat mechanical and required. To explain this, note that the ECB sets three key rates: the marginal lending facility for overnight lending *to* banks; the main refinancing rate, which is the rate at which banks can borrow *from* the ECB; and the deposit rate, which is the rate that banks receive *from* the ECB for money parked at the ECB.

To maintain a positive spread between the rate at which the banks received funds and the rate at which they deposited funds, as soon as the refinancing rate was dropped to 0.15%, the deposit rate had to go to −0.10% (to maintain the 0.25% spread). Importantly, only banks that are required to deposit the money at the ECB had to pay to deposit. At that point, few economists would have anticipated the length, depth, and duration of the negative interest rate policy or that it would transmit into the yield curve.

As presented on the ECB website, the theory is that

> consumers and businesses can borrow more cheaply and this helps stimulate economic recovery. In a market economy, the return on savings is determined by supply and demand. For example, low long-term interest rates are the result of low growth and an insufficient return on capital. The ECB's interest rate decisions will in fact benefit savers in the end because they support growth and thus create a climate in which interest rates can gradually return to higher levels.[11]

As discussed previously, this statement does not acknowledge that the ECB is one of the largest buyers of long-term bonds, and it is doing so in a magnitude that exceeds the net supply of such bonds.

To encourage borrowing for longer, the ECB has also recently introduced long-term loans called targeted longer-term refinancing operations (TLTROs).

> The targeted longer-term refinancing operations (TLTROs) are Eurosystem operations that provide financing to credit institutions. By offering banks long-term funding at attractive conditions they preserve favourable borrowing conditions for banks and stimulate bank lending to the real economy.[12]

TLTRO amounts are linked to participant banks' lending patterns (see discussion in Rasmus 2017)—that is, the banks have to loan to nonfinancial corporations and households to qualify.

Among the unconventional mechanisms to keep borrowing costs low, asset purchases are another major tactic. The ECB is now one of the largest buyers and holders of both government and corporate bonds in Europe.

---

[11]"The ECB's Negative Interest Rate," ECB website (12 June 2014), https://www.ecb.europa.eu/explainers/tell-me-more/html/why-negative-interest-rate.en.html.
[12]"Targeted Longer-Term Refinancing Operations (TLTROs)," ECB website, https://www.ecb.europa.eu/mopo/implement/omo/tltro/html/index.en.html.

Box 3: Asset Purchase Programmes

The ECB's Asset Purchase Programme (APP) is part of a package of non-standard monetary policy measures that also includes targeted longer-term refinancing operations, and which was initiated in mid-2014 to support the monetary policy transmission mechanism and provide the amount of policy accommodation needed to ensure price stability. It consists of the

- corporate sector purchase programme (CSPP)
- public sector purchase programme (PSPP)
- asset-backed securities purchase programme (ABSPP)
- third covered bond purchase programme (CBPP3)

APP Net Purchases, by Programme

Between October 2014 and December 2018 the Eurosystem conducted net purchases of securities under one or more of the asset purchase programmes. During the net asset purchase phase, monthly purchase pace averaged:

- €60 billion from March 2015 to March 2016
- €80 billion from April 2016 to March 2017
- €60 billion from April 2017 to December 2017
- €30 billion from January 2018 to September 2018
- €15 billion from October 2018 to December 2018

Between January 2019 and October 2019, the Eurosystem fully reinvested the principal payments from maturing securities held in the APP portfolios. The Governing Council aimed to maintain the size of its cumulative net purchases under each constituent programme of the APP at their respective levels as at the end of December 2018.

On 12 September 2019 the ECB Governing Council decided that "net purchases will be restarted under the Governing Council's asset purchase programme (APP) at a monthly pace of €20 billion as from 1 November 2019. The Governing Council expects them to run for as long as necessary to reinforce the accommodative impact of its policy rates, and to end shortly before it starts raising the key ECB interest rates."

Asset Purchase Programs

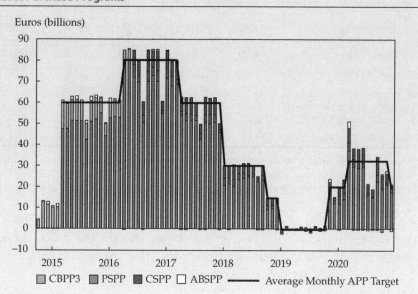

Cumulative Asset Holdings of the ECB

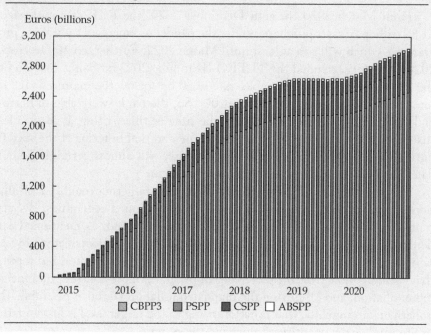

Eurosystem Holdings under the Asset Purchase Programme

Changes of holdings (previous month)	ABSPP	CBPP3	CSPP	PSPP	APP
Holdings* in November 2020	30,161	286,458	248,340	2,330,562	2,895,521
Monthly net purchases	−656	1,529	2,378	17,822	21,072
Quarter-end amortisation adjustment and redemptions of coupon STRIPS	−8	−441	−315	−6,777	−7,541
Holdings* in December 2020	29,497	287,545	250,403	2,341,607	2,909,053

*At amortised cost, in euro millions, at month-end. Figures might not add up due to rounding. Figures are preliminary and might be subject to revision.
Source: ECB website https://www.ecb.europa.eu/mopo/implement/app/html/index.en.html.

(Pursuant to Article 1(4) of Guideline (EU) 2015/510 (ECB/2014/60), the Governing Council may, at any time, change the tools, instruments, requirements, criteria and procedures for the implementation of Eurosystem monetary policy operations.)

Note: The material here was reproduced from "Asset Purchase Programmes," ECB website, https://www.ecb.europa.eu/mopo/implement/app/html/index.en.html.

From March 2020 through December 2020, the ECB also authorized €1.85 trillion of asset purchases under the pandemic emergency purchase programme, which will run at least until March 2022. Further, on 10 December 2020, the ECB extended the TLTRO III to June 2022 for banks that lend to the real economy at a "favourable" rate of 50 bps below the main refinancing rate, which in January 2021 stood at 0%. So, the banks were able to borrow and get paid for such borrowing. At the time of this writing, it seems clear that further innovations will be forthcoming and that in terms of the specific means for monetary stimulus, this monograph will almost certainly be outdated by the time it gets into the hands of readers.

To generalize, most central banks have been targeting roughly 2% inflation using "whatever it takes" in most of the developed economies. Because central bankers are predominantly PhD economists and, as mentioned earlier, have generally studied the same texts and been "indoctrinated" by the same theories, general consensus exists among them in the causal assumption that (1) more money means more consumption, (2) more consumption means more inflation, and (3) hitting the mandated inflation targets is essential. The underlying argument is that inflation rising to the target level is just a matter of time and of the quantity of money in the system.

This naturally leads to policy rates below zero once the taboo of the zero bound is broken. The theory says that if low rates encourage borrowing and spending, then "obviously," negative rates will encourage *even more* borrowing and spending. Among many criticisms of this theory, one is that perhaps the problem is not liquidity in the first place. Consumers are already saturated with excess cash to the point they might simply prefer to save the extra liquidity for the future when inflation does rise, or invest in financial assets, a possibility to which we will return in the next chapter.

Evidence is also available that the money is being pushed into the system by the ECB's massive purchases and that through negative yields, the dynamic is basically creating a deficit for peripheral countries, such as Italy and Spain, and a surplus for core countries, such as Germany. The ECB publishes TARGET2 (Trans-European Automated Real-Time Gross Settlement Express Transfer System 2) statistics, which show that as of this writing, the German Bundesbank is sitting on record positive TARGET2 balances of over €1 trillion, while Spain and Italy are running liabilities of approximately €500 billion each. One possible interpretation of this dynamic is that much of the money being created is being recycled into assets being held in Germany.

In May 2020, Germany's constitutional court ruled that the ECB's bond buying partially contravened the law because neither the German government nor the parliament signed off on the spending, to which the ECB responded that it was "more determined than ever" (Koranyi and Canepa 2020). This set up a confrontation between the ECB and the German courts that was finally settled in 2020 with the German central bank, the Bundesbank, being allowed to continue its purchases of negative-yielding German bunds.

The ECB's aggressive purchase of "eligible" corporate bonds under its four stimulus programs has resulted in a demand for more assets than are available for sale, thereby creating a sharp drop in yields of corporate bonds relative to credit default swap spreads, as noted in a recent paper co-authored by an ECB senior economist (Papoutsi and Mota 2021). Approximately 40% of the eligible corporate bonds in the corporate bond index for Europe were trading at negative yields. In other words, private companies could borrow money and be paid to do so, as long as their credit was eligible for purchase by the ECB.

The ECB's 12 September 2019 press conference showed how unintended consequences of a path-dependent policy framework can occur when traveling in uncharted territory. At this meeting, the ECB cut the deposit rate, as expected, to −0.50% from −0.40%, which was technically an "easing." The bank brought an essentially unlimited and open-ended quantitative easing program back into the picture, promising to buy €20 billion of bonds every month starting in the near future. It also introduced a tiering system for deposits, as follows: Deposits below a six-times multiple of required reserves would earn a return of 0%, whereas anything above would earn the negative interest rate, with banks having to pay money on their reserves exceeding the threshold. Leading up to and during the meeting, strong opposition to the aggressive bond-buying plan was reported from some of the member countries. In the press conference, then ECB President Draghi essentially admitted that the central bank was possibly out of ammunition and pleaded for fiscal stimulus from countries with positive fiscal balances. (See European Central Bank 2019 for the full meeting transcript.)

The impact of the small rate cut was essentially overwhelmed by the market's interpretation. After a brief and short-lived fall in yields, the German yield curve flattened and yields rose by almost 0.12% in the two-year maturity. Instead of falling, rates rose.

To understand why yields rose even as the deposit rate was cut, we have to understand the interaction of the public sector policy and the profit maximization impulse of the private sector—in this case, European banks. From the perspective of a bank with excess deposits, finding a bank that did not have deposits above the six-times threshold and moving the money there at a 0% interest rate probably made sense. In other words, the introduction of the tier within the very heterogeneous European banking system created an arbitrage for banks. When the deposit rate is −0.50% and the two-year yield is −0.75%, it makes sense for investors to consider selling these two-year bonds and moving into bonds that yield higher than −0.50%, or even depositing the money at banks with reserves yielding 0%. The most important beneficiaries of the "easing" were such peripheral countries as Italy, where longer-term yields fell significantly in the aftermath of the ECB's aggressive actions.

As of this writing, yields in the United States are still positive on Treasury bonds. If we plotted the 10-Year Treasury yield from the birth of the United States to date, the trend would clearly show that we could be extremely close to yields in the United States breaking the 0% barrier if there is another large and unanticipated economic shock. Although Fed officials have recently said that negative interest rates in the United States are not likely, the market has tended not to believe such pronouncements. Indeed, 0% interest rate floors have traded in the market. The general perception is that even if the Fed were to not go below zero, any shocks to the economy could result in the perception of deflation. But it is also possible that central banks have simply become helpless accelerators of a long, secular trend of falling yields because of other reasons, such as the following:

1. The old age dependency ratio is increasing, and demographic changes are resulting in more savings.

2. An increase in research and technology, or the "Amazonification" of many traditional business models, could result in a deflationary impact.

3. Globalization has increased (e.g., see Gygli, Haelg, Potrafke, and Sturm 2019).

4. Real growth volatility has fallen, resulting in a lower required duration premium.

5. Economic policy uncertainty has risen, resulting in precautionary holdings of debt.

According to this view, if another major recession occurs and globalization goes in reverse, US yields can easily go negative, despite the Fed's opposition (at least as of this writing) to negative yields. Indeed, from a very long-term perspective, yields in the United States appear to be a whisker away from falling below zero in the longer historical context, although opinions exist that the coordinated inflationary policy of global central banks, if successful, could turn the decades long trend in the other direction.

For readers who survived the extremely deep dive into the discussion of the ECB in this chapter, the reward is a recognition that we are in uncharted waters when it comes to monetary policy, regardless of the technical nature of many of the theories that are invoked to justify or criticize current monetary policy stance. Skeptics might argue that policy is being created in real time. Like the famous "whack-a-mole" game, the consequences of something going wrong in the causal, almost mechanical structure envisioned by policymakers could be devastating for the economy. For financial markets, the consequences are thankfully a little bit more transparent, and to this discussion we turn in the next chapter.

6. Consequences for Asset Valuation and Risk Management

> "That is about all I have learned—to study general conditions, to take a position and stick to it."
>
> —*Edwin LeFevre*, Reminiscences of a Stock Operator

Asset price targeting is not an explicit part of the mandate for most central banks, but it has been an implicit target of policymaking for a very long time. Veteran investors summarize this observation succinctly as "Don't fight the Fed." For the Federal Reserve, financial stability is part of the unofficial mandate, and most people would agree that a large shock to the financial markets and asset prices can adversely affect the official mandate of "full employment and stable prices" by affecting financial stability, which could result in illiquidity, fear, and even market panics.

Here is an excerpt from the May 2020 *Financial Stability Report*:[13]

> Promoting financial stability is a key element in meeting the Federal Reserve's dual mandate for monetary policy regarding full employment and stable prices. In an unstable financial system, adverse events are more likely to result in severe financial stress and disrupt the flow of credit, leading to high unemployment and great financial hardship. Monitoring and assessing financial stability also support the Federal Reserve's regulatory and supervisory activities, which promote the safety and soundness of our nation's banks and other important financial institutions. Information gathered while monitoring the stability of the financial system helps the Federal Reserve develop its view of the salient risks to be included in the scenarios of the stress tests and its setting of the countercyclical capital buffer (CCyB). (Board of Governors of the Federal Reserve System 2020a, p. 1)

As market participants have learned, asset prices are being more explicitly targeted by all central banks today, even though asset prices are not yet part of the official mandate. The Bank of Japan buys equities via ETFs, the ECB and the Federal Reserve buy government and corporate bonds, and the Fed, in the aftermath of the COVID-19 crisis, also buys increasing amounts of corporate bonds, high-yield (junk) bonds and ETFs, and asset-backed securities.

So, how exactly does central bank policy influence asset prices? To answer this question, we have to go back to the fundamental building blocks of all asset pricing mentioned earlier. All asset prices are some kind of expected

---

[13]https://www.federalreserve.gov/publications/files/financial-stability-report-20200515.pdf.

present value calculation of future cash flows. In other words, the price P of any future cash flow c (which can be fixed or contingent) to be received in time T, when the continuously compounded yield is y, can be written as[14]

$$P = ce^{-yT}.$$

If the yield is negative, then the pricing function grows with time and does so in an exponential or "explosive" fashion. In other words, the more negative the yields, the higher the present value of an unknown cash flow; moreover, the present value becomes higher than the future value. For instance, if the value at maturity is US$100 and the yield is negative, the present value is higher than US$100. This inverted time value of money affects every asset's price because the discount function is fundamental to all asset pricing. If investors interpret lending for longer as a negative expected return choice, they would be induced to invest in riskier short-term assets or to just spend the money rather than saving it. In other words, the premium they could potentially earn by investing for longer will be less attractive. These decisions are not purely mathematical but also rely on underlying economic expectations and on attitudes toward time and risk.

The Term Premium

Our logical starting point, then, is the term premium (i.e., the premium demanded by an investor for engaging in longer-maturity investments and taking on increased duration risk).

To extract the term premium, we use a very simple two-factor "affine" model, specified by two yield curve factors, which captures the essential features of the yield curve relevant to our discussion in the context of the underlying economics. (An affine model is one in which zero-coupon bond prices are related to the spot interest rate in a relatively simple way, so that observing prices in the market allows the dynamics that drive the term structure to be easily extracted in terms of a small number of variables and parameters.) The variables in this model have a natural mapping to inflation, growth, and monetary policy metrics, and with some tedious but routine stochastic calculus, the model can be solved in closed form (see Bhansali 2007). The building block of all term structure models is the short rate. In the present case, the relevant short rate is the deposit rate, shown in **Exhibit 14**. While simpler or

---

[14]In what to some readers might be the more familiar discrete-time notation, the present value or price, P, is approximated by $\dfrac{c}{(1+y)^t}$.

Exhibit 14. ECB Deposit Facility Announcement Rate: EUORDEPO Index

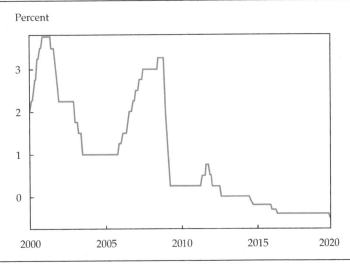

Percent

Source: Bloomberg Finance L.P.

more complex models can surely be constructed, we find a two-factor model to be complex enough, but not too complex, to explain the dynamics of the shape of the yield curve. These dynamics are essential to understanding the influence of the central banks on the term premium directly and thus on all asset prices indirectly.

The two-factor model is specified by two latent stochastic factors x and y and a deterministic factor z. The evolution is specified by the coupled equations

$$dx = \mu dt + \sigma_x dw_x,$$

$$dy = -\alpha y dt + \sigma_y dw_y, \quad \text{and}$$

$$dz = k(x + y - z)dt.$$

Intuitively, the long-term factor x represents the fundamental structure of the economy (we can think of this factor as related to inflation, which is the principal factor driving long-term yields), and the spread factor y represents mean-reverting transitory fluctuations (we can think of this factor as loosely related to growth) that are pulled back toward the long-term mean of y. The central bank (the ECB, in our example) controls the short-term rate z near its equilibrium value of $x + y$ in a locally deterministic manner. The parameters σ_x and σ_y are volatilities in basis points per year. Because the processes are normal, negative realizations for both the factors and the short-term rate are allowed, thereby allowing for negative interest rates, which a lognormal model of interest rates would not allow.

Our interest is in estimating the term premium given by μ as well as the value for the fundamental factors x and y. We can solve the model analytically, and the resultant nonlinear functions for the yields of zero-coupon bonds can be fitted to observed yields to extract the values for the key variables.[15]

In **Exhibit 15**, we display the fits for the four variables obtained by fitting the closed-form solution for yields in the model to the yield data.

Further, **Exhibit 16** illustrates the implication of the model for all instantaneous forward short-term rates for maturities from one year out to 30 years.

Exhibits 14 to 16 clearly show that the impact of the declining level of short-term rates, "forward guidance," and bond purchases by the ECB has been to drive expectations of forward rates at all maturities below zero. However, interestingly, the term premium in this admittedly naive model of the term structure, as illustrated in Panel D of Exhibit 15, has not declined by much. Even as short-term rates have been driven way below zero, the required compensation for extending duration risk has remained high enough. In other words, by lending at a less negative yield and borrowing at a more negative yield, investors can earn a "premium," inducing investors to hold longer-term bonds despite negative yields, as long as the financing cost is more negative than the negative rate at which investments are made!

How do negative rates influence compounded returns? Note that just by applying the simple formula $FV = (1 + y)^n PV$ relating future value (FV) to present value (PV), we can deduce that for a negative yield of 1% and inflation of 2%, the real value of US$1 falls to only 40 cents in 30 years and to five cents in 100 years (see **Exhibit 17**)! In other words, by investing at negative yields, the investor does not earn any "real" premium but actually pays for perceived safety of principal, negligible as it might be in real terms. As discussed earlier, this loss of premium for principal protection is a hallmark of an option.

---

[15]To estimate the model, we fix the parameters $\sigma_x = 0.0091, \alpha = 0.5, \sigma_y = 0.0155, k = 2$ and use the zero-coupon yield levels for the German yield curve going back to 2000. The Bloomberg tickers for the yields are as follows: EUORDEPO Index for the deposit rate, GTDEM2Y Corp for the two-year yield, GTDEM5Y Corp for the five-year yield, GTDEM10Y Corp for the 10-year yield, and GTDEM30Y Corp for the 30-year yield. The time-series evolutions of the variables are displayed in the exhibits.

Exhibit 15.   Fits for *x*, *y*, *z*, and μ from 2000 to 2019 for the German Sovereign Bond Market Yield Curve

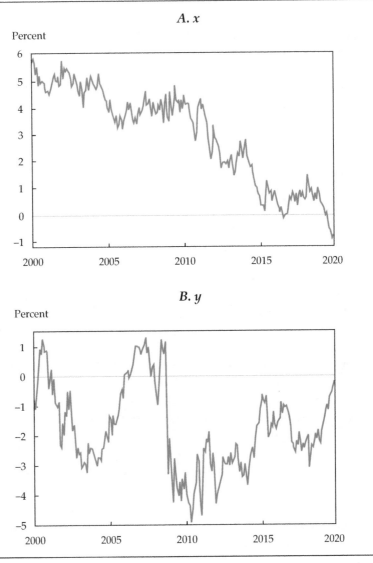

A. *x*

B. *y*

(continued)

Exhibit 15. Fits for *x, y, z,* and μ from 2000 to 2019 for the German Sovereign Bond Market Yield Curve (*continued*)

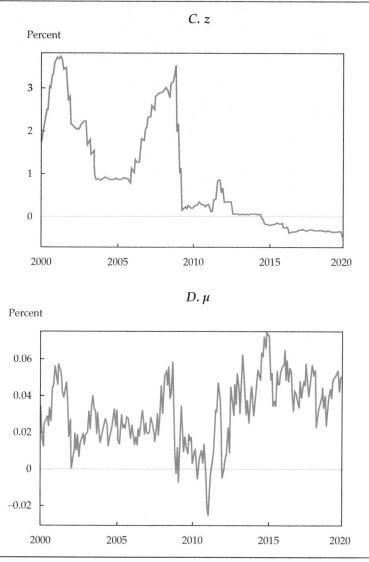

Note: The vertical axes in these charts correspond to the values of the latent factors in the affine models that drive the bond price dynamics.
Source: LongTail Alpha, LLC.

Exhibit 16. Implied Instantaneous Forward Rates for Different Maturities from 2000 to 2019 for the German Sovereign Bond Market Yield Curve

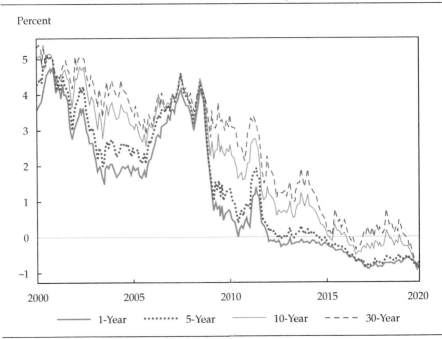

Sources: Bloomberg Finance L.P., LongTail Alpha, LLC.

Exhibit 17. Future Value of US$1 for Varying Maturity and Yield Levels

		Years				
	US$1	1	10	30	50	100
	5.00%	$1.05	$1.63	$4.32	$11.47	$131.50
	2.00%	1.02	1.22	1.81	2.69	7.24
	0.50%	1.01	1.05	1.16	1.28	1.65
Yield	0.00%	1.00	1.00	1.00	1.00	1.00
	−0.50%	1.00	0.95	0.86	0.78	0.61
	−1.00%	0.99	0.90	0.74	0.61	0.37
	−3.00%	0.97	0.74	0.40	0.22	0.05

Source: Author.

This is an interesting and consequential conclusion because the term structure of interest rates is a building block of the discount factor for all assets and as such is likely to influence the pricing of other, long-duration assets, such as equities and real estate. To the degree that the term structure has the embedded negative expected return and time-decay characteristics of an option, all assets that use this building block would suffer as the value of the optionality dissipates over time. However, for the moment, the rapid fall in interest rates and yields has affected most asset prices in a positive way.

Impact on the Stock Market

The market pays attention to what is known as the "Fed model," which evaluates the relative cheapness of equities over bonds by comparing the earnings yield of the stock market to the yield on long-term bonds (e.g., the yield on the 10-year maturity US Treasury). As the Fed bought more long-term bonds and corporate securities to keep yields and spreads low, the earnings yield of the equity market began to look high relative to history, thereby implying that equities were cheap even as they made record highs in the middle of the COVID-19 crisis. Indeed, the Fed's own November 2020 *Financial Stability Report* had this to say about the performance and relative attractiveness of equities:

> Equity prices rose sharply, with higher valuations supported, in part, by low interest rates[.]

> Valuations in equity markets have risen substantially as equity prices have continued to move up since the previous *Financial Stability Report*. Prices relative to forecasts of corporate earnings have also risen considerably and are currently near the top of their historical distribution, even though there is significant uncertainty in the earnings outlook among market participants . . . . However, while the gap between the forward earnings-to-price ratio and the expected real yield on 10-year Treasury securities—a rough measure of the premium that investors require for holding risky corporate equities—has declined since May, it remains above its historical median due to the low level of Treasury yields . . . . This development suggests that investor risk appetite, though higher since May, is still within historical norms. (Board of Governors of the Federal Reserve System 2020b, p. 19)

As of early 2020, according to a Goldman Sachs report published 20 February 2020, the capitalization of the US equity market was approximately US$50 trillion. Of this, households owned approximately US$17 trillion, 34% of the total. Actively managed mutual funds owned US$11.5 trillion, 23% of the total. Thus, households plus active mutual funds owned US$28.5 trillion, 57% of the total. Foreign investors owned

US$7.5 trillion, 15% of the total, and defined benefit pension funds owned US$6.0 trillion, 12% of the total. Further, ETFs owned US$3.0 trillion, 6% of the total; business holdings and family offices owned US$2.0 trillion, 4% of the total; and hedge funds owned US$1.5 trillion, 3% of the total.

A perception by retail investors (i.e., households and indexed mutual funds) that equities are cheap relative to the artificially suppressed interest rates could therefore result in a significant amount of capital inflow into the stock market. By reducing interest rates across the term structure by a relatively small amount, central banks can engineer a substantial inflow of capital into risky assets in the short run, purely by appealing to relative value between asset classes. By providing low interest rate conditions as a promise along with actually offering loans at no cost, they can also facilitate a natural and "optimal" response by retail investors, who are the largest participants in the stock market, to pile into growth stocks, especially those that are most levered to low interest rates, provide no income or dividends, and have recent positive price momentum. I will have more to say about this toward the end of this chapter, where I discuss the recent interest in call options on speculative stocks by retail investors.

Thus, one of the consequences of negative interest rates and yields is that investors looking for return have moved into equity assets where there is still some hope of positive total return. The total return of all assets is increasingly driven by price appreciation because there is very little dividend income. This low income return is a direct result of the high stock prices caused by the impact of low interest rates on the present-value calculation. In a world where capital can flee from areas where yields are low and/or negative to areas where they can be invested in other assets, substantial asset price increases can result.

History is full of examples of similar behavior. Many past stock market bubbles have been born and grown out of easy money and the crowding out of investors from low-returning bond markets into risky assets. The South Sea Bubble of 1720 grew out of a scheme, backed by the government, to persuade the holders of almost all the new government debt to exchange their government obligations for shares in a semiofficial trading company, the South Sea Company. South Sea stock appreciated that year from £128 in January 1720 to £1,000 a share in the middle of 1720. By November of that year, the bubble had burst, and South Sea stock was back to £135. As a result, the Chancellor of the Exchequer was imprisoned, and the Bubble Act was passed, which restricted the formation of new companies (Homer and Sylla 2005).

As the total size of the bond markets has grown rapidly as a result of increased supply, the demand from government institutions has met or exceeded this supply—partly because the government has been buying up the extra supply to keep yields low, and partly because of the emergence of captive buyers who are required to buy these bonds. We have discussed how pension funds and insurance companies are captive buyers of long-term bonds regardless of yield levels. As yields fall, it also becomes more profitable for corporations to buy back their stock by issuing debt at lower yields, thereby creating demand for equity that might exceed the supply of equity (de-equitization).

Over the past decade of easing of policy rates, the equity supply has reduced significantly because of both buybacks and the search for assets with positive expected returns. Thus, we can see how a decline in interest rates influences all assets, not just the bond market. One can argue that a key tenet of asset allocation (i.e., forecasting returns) has now become an exercise in forecasting how long interest rates will stay negative or very low so that such dynamics can continue to prevail.

Asset allocation depends on diversification across assets to mitigate risk, and the influence of common factors on all assets reduces the potential diversification benefits from buying different types of assets. Because the discount factor is common to all assets, any unanticipated upward shock to rates would be likely to affect all assets simultaneously. In other words, the natural diversification benefits of having multiple assets in a portfolio can be overwhelmed by a simultaneous decline in the price of all assets driven by an interest rate increase. It would not be surprising for continued central bank stimulus to result in a sudden, unanticipated rise in inflationary expectations, which would in turn cause investors to expect drastically higher rates and then cause stock and bond prices to decline simultaneously.

A very important second consideration emerges from the action of investors searching for yield in a low-yield environment. As discussed in Bhansali and Harris (2018), the need for yield and income generation resulted in the development of an ecosystem of "short volatility" strategies that can be collectively dubbed "shadow insurance" and short volatility speculation. The commonality between many of these strategies is that they are all contingent on selling volatility via implicit or explicit options. As a result, such option selling could run the risk of overwhelming the liquid derivatives markets if the risk management–driven delta-hedging activity is correlated and simultaneous. We saw this effect in the sharp unwind of the XIV short volatility exchange-traded note (ETN) in February 2018.

A destabilizing shock can result in many participants in the short volatility ecosystem exiting or attempting to hedge using liquid equity index futures. As one example, a cascade of selling during February–March 2020 resulted in many short volatility and risk premium strategies suffering huge losses.

Finally, other, unanticipated consequences can emerge. For instance, as discussed earlier, a consequence of negative interest rates in Europe and

Japan, when combined with the positive interest rates in the United States, was that the short-term interest rate differential, US buyers began to prefer even negative-yielding bonds in Europe on a currency-hedged basis and foreign investors began to shun higher-yielding US dollar bonds.

This cross-currency bond holding strategy embodies a highly levered cross-border yield curve and cross-currency leverage because a negative-yielding bond is held primarily for the benefit offered by the currency hedging, which has to be rolled on a short-term basis. Anecdotally, in the winter of 2019, overnight funding rates in the United States spiked to 10%, which had been unheard of since the global financial crisis. With all the money being printed by global central banks, how could dealers, who set the overnight funding rates, not be able to finance their holdings of Treasuries overnight at reasonable rates? This "repo problem" was in part a symptom of large interest rate differentials between the United States and the rest of the world due to persistently negative interest rates in Europe and Japan, which caused traditional buyers of US Treasuries (i.e., foreigners) to hesitate from buying Treasuries because it cost them carry to do so on a currency-hedged basis.

One other consequence of negative yields is that the net present value of longer-dated cash flows is boosted as rates go negative. For example, let us say that we are given a choice of US$1 in one year or US$1 in 30 years. This would be typical, for instance, when comparing the present value of a dividend-paying stock to that of a non-dividend-paying growth stock. If all rates and yields are minus 1%, the value today of the US$1 one year from now is US$1.01, but the value today of the $1 in 30 years is US$1.35 (assuming continuous compounding). So, just as a practical matter, all else being equal, an investor would prefer to pay more for the growth in the future. This shows up in a comparison of the returns to the growth factor versus the value factor, with growth significantly outperforming value during a period of low and declining interest rates.

De-Equitization: Buybacks and Stock Scarcity

When the cost of issuing debt is low, it makes sense for corporations to issue more debt to buy their stock back. Corporate debt is tax deductible in the United States (with certain exceptions), while dividend payments from equities are taxable for the equity owners. Increasing equity prices and falling net equity outstanding can also result in a cycle of perception that the firms are on better footing and that the decreasing number of shares could be EPS (earnings per share) enhancing.

Stock buybacks increased rapidly after the global financial crisis, as can be seen in **Exhibit 18**. As long as a company's forward or expected earnings

Exhibit 18.   Stock Buybacks and Earnings Yield

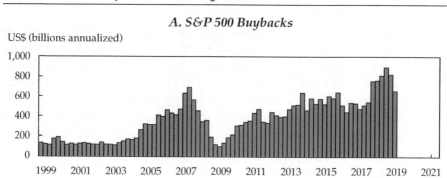

A. S&P 500 Buybacks

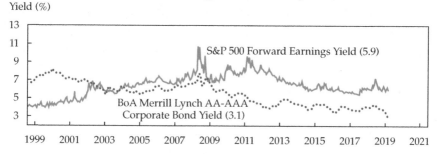

B. S&P 500 Forward Earnings Yield and Corporate Bond Yield

Note: Forward earnings (time-weighted average of consensus operating earnings estimates for current and next year) divided by S&P 500 stock price index.
Source: Yardeni Research Inc. Used with permission.

yield is much higher than corporate bond yields, the holders of equity can capture the spread between them by issuing bonds and buying back stock. We also have to recognize that senior management is in many cases compensated for share performance, in the form of options grants. This creates an incentive to increase share prices via buybacks rather than producing the same return to shareholders by paying dividends.

That share price increases result in buybacks to make compensation payments to holders of stock options is a fact (Yardeni and Abbott 2019), but that fact still allows for the principle that any market purchase of stock leads to an increase in the price. In the aftermath of the 2020 COVID-19 crisis, the Federal Reserve started to buy corporate bonds directly and via ETFs, including bonds of such companies as Microsoft that were delivering record profits. Given the low level of yields, tech stocks not surprisingly continued to hit new highs despite the catastrophic shock to the economy. Also unsurprising is that buybacks are making a comeback as of this writing, given the extremely low cost to finance buybacks.

In 2019, a Citibank research report estimated that the cost of equity in the United States was 6.7% versus 4.1% for debt (comparable numbers for Europe not including the United Kingdom were 5.4% and 2.0%, respectively; for the United Kingdom, 7.6% and 3.0%; and for Japan, 4.6% and 0.4%) (Citi Equity Research 2019). A corollary of this observation is that cheap debt financing has found its way into private equity, where venture funds are flush with extra liquidity and can satisfy the need for liquidity from startups and younger firms.

Indeed, "tech unicorns," which are firms that rapidly reach billion-dollar-plus valuations based on cheap private equity financing, are everywhere. Tech firms in the United States have been buying back more equity than they are issuing, explaining a good part of the outperformance of the tech sector. One example is Booking Holdings, which many know as the original Priceline.com. From the summer of 1999 to 2003, and coinciding with the tech bubble bursting, the stock price for Booking (at that time called Priceline) declined from US$700 per share to below US$7. In 2000 alone, the stock declined 97.23% (Bloomberg).

The stock rallied as of the end of 2020 to a price of US$2,227 (i.e., a gain of almost 10,000%)! Although this company has had solid earnings growth, looking at the financial reports, one sees that the company has been putting a lot of its cash flow into buying back its stock. On average, Booking has been buying back approximately US$1 billion of shares per quarter for the past five years. This is approximately 5% of the total outstanding value of the shares per year. Since 2014, the share count for Booking has fallen from 52 million to 42 million shares, a reduction of almost 20% (Bloomberg).

Another example is Apple. Since 2014, and coinciding with low borrowing costs and the popularity of its products, Apple has reduced its share count by over 25%, and its valuation has increased from approximately US$400 billion to almost US$2.1 trillion (as of February 2021).

How Negative Yields Can Create Instability: The Rise of Shadow Financial Reinsurance

The XIV debacle of 2018 resulted in many "short volatility" ETNs imploding. Like the global financial crisis of 2008–2009, this development was one of the unintended consequences of low yields. Low levels of implied volatility that emanated from systematic yield enhancement strategies, such as volatility selling, created massive financial instability.

The prevalence of structured investment vehicles (SIVs) is blamed to some degree for the ultimate unwind of credit leverage in 2007. In simple terms, an SIV is a shadow bank that borrowed short and lent long, not unlike what a bank does, or borrowed at lower-risk interest rates and lent out at higher-risk rates to generate yield in an otherwise low-yield environment. By doing so, SIVs operated under the radar of bank regulators and captured both the term spread and the credit spread.

Because this maturity and credit transformation was so appealing for the initial participants, it attracted others looking for the same "free" money, until the market became so large that it eventually imploded from within. Of course, as we now know, the underlying (faulty) assumption that drove this excess was that the value of the collateral (i.e., the housing market) would never go down very much. Given the financial engineering of the times, one could operate a levered vehicle, such as a shadow bank, with minimal infrastructure and cost (and certainly not a bank charter) as long as someone was available to provide funds that could be loaned out or invested.

By 2018, shadow banks had been replaced with what we can loosely call "shadow financial insurance companies." When an investor sells an option, whether through the explicit sale of put options or call options or through products that prepackage such insurance, the investor is essentially selling insurance against large market moves. The underlying (again, somewhat faulty) assumption is that over time, the seller of insurance always gets to keep a risk premium over the true value of the insurance.

In a world where one cannot see volatility rising because of rising equity markets, just as one could not forecast that housing prices would ever go down, operating such an insurance-selling operation is perfectly rational because it is a positive expected return strategy over time. It might even make sense to diversify the insurance-selling business by operating like a multiline insurer, selling insurance across all asset classes and maturities. But levered insurance selling creates massive financial instability.

Just as an investor can use the derivatives markets to operate a virtual refinery out of his bedroom (e.g., by selling gasoline futures and buying crude oil futures), an investor with access to the options markets could operate a virtual insurance company by buying an inverse volatility ETF, such as XIV or SVXY. Indeed, an investor who buys one of these products listed on the exchanges is entering into a contract whereby the provider of the security goes out as an agent and sells VIX futures in an amount exactly matched to produce the payoff pattern from selling volatility. Just as the SIV was a sophisticated bit of financial engineering to bring credit and term structure arbitrage to the masses, volatility ETFs and ETNs brought volatility selling—up to then an institutional activity—to the masses.

In the case of the SIV, multiple layers of financial engineering are worth dissecting. In the first step, a loan finances the home purchase. In the second step, loans are pooled together into a security. In the third step, derivatives (e.g., credit default swaps) are built on the pooled loan security. Finally, the derivatives are sliced, or "tranched," and put into the SIVs that finance the purchase through borrowing. In the four-step process, the risks of the ultimate underlying asset, the price of the house, are levered multiple times, and each rung in the ladder becomes increasingly sensitive to housing price fluctuations. As housing prices rose, the mathematical expectation of the tranches not being able to pay off diminished, thereby creating more interest and demand and an increasing appearance of safety. But later, as housing prices fell, the inverse happened, and the tranches fell, in many cases to zero, thereby wiping out demand.

Now let us track the financial engineering steps involved with an inverse volatility ETF, which in many ways was similar (including the uncanny similarity in name). First, there is an underlying security, which is the stock of a large cap company. In the second step, many such stocks are pooled together into an index (e.g., the S&P 500 Index). In the third step, derivatives on the index, such as call and put options, are designed and traded. In the fourth step, an index of all the put and call options is constructed (e.g., the VIX) based on a formula. Because the VIX itself is not tradable, in the fifth step, a new, tradable derivative, the VIX futures contract, is constructed with the VIX as its basis. In the final step, a security is constructed on the VIX futures contracts; such securities include the VXX, XIV, and SVXY, all of which trade on the stock exchanges and can be bought and sold as one would a stock.

As should be clear at this stage, financial engineering technology has taken a plain vanilla security and, by slicing, dicing, and repackaging its cash flows multiple times, created another security that is a highly levered and option-laden version of the first-generation security. This engineered security trades on the exchanges under the same rules as the original stocks, even though it is an extremely levered version of the initial security. The primary purpose of this type of strategy is to convert option sale premiums into yield.

As anticipated in one of my papers written before the XIV implosion (Bhansali and Harris 2018), the risk to such a house of cards is that any one of the links in the financial engineering turns out to be a weak one. The most obvious trigger is a severe decline in the stock market as a whole. Again, while it is true that even a small move in the price of housing could have brought the SIVs, and indeed the credit markets, to a crash in 2008, the real risk was not a sustained housing market downturn but the forced selling of the securities built at the top of the financial engineering pyramid. As these top-level securities were sold at fire sale prices (e.g., during the liquidation of the Bear Stearns hedge funds), each rung in the ladder weakened, and one could argue that as the spigot of easy credit was turned off, the housing market suffocated and prices started to fall.

Whether the housing market crash created the global financial crisis or the failure of levered securities created the housing market crash is an unsatisfying question to study because either one would eventually have resulted in the other. Just the act of dynamic risk management could start such a cascade, as was observed in the spring of 2020. So, for a system levered to low yields, the real risk is that for some unforecastable reason, volatility and fear rise and create a set of cascading shocks that ultimately results in the equity markets falling sharply.

This situation could be triggered by an event that creates a large amount of uncertainty. An unexpected negative or positive event could lead to a large shock to, say, the VIX, or to the volatility of interest rates. As a result, some of the systematic volatility selling strategies ("shadow insurance companies") back off from selling insurance or maybe even buy back their insurance contracts at a higher price for safety. Tracing the financial engineering just described backward, the provider of the packaged insurance security then buys back the VIX futures or the short volatility derivatives. As the expected level of the VIX rises, arbitrageurs bid up the prices of the options (i.e., the actual value of the VIX increases). At this stage, a number of mechanical strategies that use the VIX as a major input parameter—such as volatility targeting, trend following, risk parity, and others that are in many institutional portfolios and are levered to low interest rates—are triggered to reduce their exposure by design.

The way many of these strategies work is that they sell equity futures as volatility rises. If many of these strategies trigger selling at the same time, or even in a sequential manner, pressure is put on the equity index futures markets, which then, by the mechanism of arbitrage, forces actual selling of index stocks. As the stocks sell off, other markets, such as high yield and corporate credit, start to feel the impact, with their spreads widening, and force liquidations from holders of credit. As credit becomes less available, further liquidation happens. In the worst-case scenario, this shock cascades across markets and regions, and the rising liquidation and risk aversion spreads like it did in the global financial crisis until a lender of last resort steps in and stops the liquidation as soon as it threatens systemic instability.

This exact story played out, as it has countless times in the past, in March 2020 as COVID-19 became a global pandemic and resulted in economic activity coming to a standstill. The response of central banks was also as expected; with a slight delay, they embarked on a massive injection of liquidity and reduction in yields, which of course sets up increasing demand for structures and instruments that can provide yield, potentially starting another cycle of volatility-selling strategies clothed in a different type of package.

Impact on the Banking Sector

The banking model generally depends on lending for longer maturities and financing the loans with short-term borrowing. Thus, implicit in the banking model is a yield curve "carry" strategy. When yields are very low, the interest income from loans negatively affects bank profits. When the yield curve is flatter, the carry from lending long and borrowing short is lower, thereby negatively affecting banking profits. Finally, when yields are negative, banks are not able to uniformly pass the negative yield to their customers. Thus, all else being equal, one of the victims of negative yields has been the banking sector. In Europe, both core and peripheral banks have been severely affected. To alleviate the problem somewhat, the ECB has resorted to new inventions, such as a tiering system for loans above a certain threshold where the banks do not have to pay a fee to keep assets at the ECB, with unintended consequences as discussed in the previous chapter.

More recently, the ECB has allowed banks to borrow at special rates that are even more negative than the bond yields at which they are lending. In other words, by giving banks money to buy bonds, the banks are guaranteed some risk-free profit, while at the same time creating a bid that would likely not exist if not for the negative-yielding bonds, but disincentivizing the banks to remain competitive.

Comparing US banks with European banks illustrates how the shape of the yield curve can influence this sector. US banks were quick to re-equitize after the global financial crisis, and in recent years they have been de-equitizing. Between 2016 and 2019, the US banking sector's stock market indexes returned approximately 31%, and the European banking sector's market indexes lost approximately 15% (Citi Equity Research 2019). In Europe, as discussed earlier, negative long-term yields and negative interest rates cannot be passed to depositors directly, meaning that the banking sector has lost one of its main sources of income. The effect of low yields is therefore twofold: Low yields make earning an income harder, so to keep enough capital to meet various requirements, more equity is issued, creating a demand–supply mismatch and potentially even more adverse leverage.

Impact on Derivatives Markets: The Resurgence of Equity Call Options

As discussed, one direct outcome of low interest rates and quantitative easing is excess liquidity in the markets. Since the global financial crisis, we have seen significant (sixfold since the lows of 2008!) gains in the equity markets, despite the sharp COVID-19 sell-off and subsequent rebound in 2020. Low interest rates, combined with the ability to lever and an implicit guarantee of the central bank "put," create optimal conditions for melt-ups in the stock market (see Bhansali 2018). In this section, I will explore in detail how low yields have the potential of making call options the preferred vehicle for speculators looking for asymmetric returns in the stock market.

Call options on the stock market, especially on stocks of companies that are highly levered to low interest rates (e.g., those in the tech sector), have become increasingly attractive for speculation. Because options provide leverage and an asymmetric payoff profile in one neat package, market participants have realized the benefits of participating in melt-ups by using call options. Further, as option trading has become more democratized and inexpensive via platforms such as Robinhood, toward the end of 2020, options markets were beginning to drive stock prices. This phenomenon is akin to, and a mirror image of, the option-driven meltdown we discussed earlier regarding destabilization emanating from the liquidation of short volatility strategies.

De-equitization, leverage, and an implicit monetary and fiscal guarantee are also all environmental variables that encourage speculation using call options. Theoretically, if we model a company's stock as a call option on its assets (including intellectual property and market adoption), then a call option on the stock is a compound call option on these assets—that is, a very highly levered derivative structure whose economic value increases with falling yields.

To understand the leverage embedded in call options, we can derive the leverage provided from the price of a call option for a non-dividend-paying stock, such as an internet stock. The Black–Scholes price of a call option, as usual, is

$$C = SN(d_1) - e^{-rt}KN(d_2),$$

where

$$d_1 = \frac{1}{\sigma\sqrt{T}}\left[\log\left(\frac{S}{K}\right) + \left(r + \frac{\sigma^2}{2}\right)T\right] \quad \text{and}$$

$$d_2 = d_1 - \sigma\sqrt{T}.$$

The equivalent value of shares of stock held when implementing the strategy using call options is simply the delta of the option, given by $N(d_1)$ times the price of the stock: $SN(d_1)$. The amount borrowed is the second term in the Black–Scholes equation, $e^{-rT}KN(d_2)$. Thus, the implicit leverage in a call option is equal to $e^{-rT}\left(\dfrac{K}{S}\right)\dfrac{N(d_2)}{N(d_1)}$. We can see that all else being equal, the impact of falling r is to boost the leverage because of the exponential discounting factor.

When the potential exists for large melt-up "right tails" due to negative rates and the search for return, call options can prove to be tempting relative to simply buying and holding stocks. Much ink has flowed in academic journals on the naiveté of investors who buy options to protect their downside risk via puts or replace the outright purchase of securities with call options. The usual arguments are supported by backward-looking analyses of options markets where the options are passively held over some fixed horizon, usually use the S&P 500 as the underlying asset being traded, and in most cases, conclude that *on average*, buying any options (call options in particular) does not make sense.

Many traditional academic theories hold that buying and holding options is a negative expected return strategy over a given fixed horizon and is good only for hedging some other position. But despite all these studies, which are fairly well known to most institutional investors, the options markets continue to grow, and investors happily and profitably part with a small premium to obtain the value of risk transfer to parties who are willing to assume the risk for a price. Further, many such theories rely on the theoretical assumption that because one can replicate a call option using a "delta" equivalent equity exposure on an almost continuous basis, call options are largely redundant. But this assumption fails when large, unhedgeable jump moves occur in the markets that could result from an excess demand for financial assets. As already discussed, one consequence of low interest rates and funding costs is a reduction in the total amount of equity, resulting in fewer shares available to hedge short call option positions.

Under these economic and market conditions, the purchase of both put and call options can be optimal for investors, and the additional convexity that only options markets can provide results in superior portfolio outcomes. In a world of tightly coupled markets, massive central bank asset purchases, instant news feeds, and the presence of technologically advanced trading "bots," both left and right tails will become a permanent fixture of investment markets. When an investor thinks about buying an option, he is making a conscious trade-off between limited loss and the possibility of time decay on the one hand, and unlimited gain as well as benefit from rising perceptions of risk on the other hand. In other words, purchasing an option instead of the underlying is an implicit bet on volatility-driven mispricing, which tends to get larger when there are jumps, uncertainty, and the possibility of new regimes of illiquidity.

Here is a cherry-picked example: On 1 September 2017, with the S&P 500 trading at 2,471, the price of a 5% out-of-the-money call, with strike 2,594 with one year left to expiry, was 2.67%. This option had a theoretical Black–Scholes delta of 0.33, and the implied volatility for that strike at that time was 12.14%. Compare this to an outright exposure to the underlying at the same time. To equalize the linear exposures, approximately three times as large an option position would need to be bought.

On 2 January 2018, the price of the same option, after accounting for time decay, was 6.45%, with a reference S&P 500 Index value of 2,691 and an implied volatility of 14%. Even as the market rallied, the implied volatility of the fixed strike put increased because of the put–call skew, because by put–call parity, in-the-money calls inherit the volatility of the out-of-the-money puts of the same strike. The index thus returned 8.91% over the four-month period. The option lost four months of time value, but despite the time decay, on an equal delta basis, it delivered 10.88% marked-to-market return, handily beating the linear equivalent on a risk-adjusted basis.

Clearly, the reason the call option in this cherry-picked example outperformed the underlying index was that the *ex ante* probability distribution, as implied by the options markets, was incorrect in pricing the probability of such a large move in the underlying. And when policy action asymmetrically tilts the return distribution, large market moves could happen, and the inherent nonlinearity of an option magnifies returns.

When major economic and market forces are at work and large, nonlinear jumps are possible, using the implied probability distribution from traded options prices can be erroneous. Major policy changes, such as the US tax reform in 2017, massive central bank support, negative yields, and trillions of dollars of fiscal stimulus, have the potential to create such nonlinearity. When combined with increased "retailization" and low-cost trading of options via new online platforms, the potential for large movements in the equity markets becomes even more likely. Other supporting reasons as to why upside optionality might be more relevant today than any time in recent memory include the following:

- *Influence of the trend toward passive products:* The move from active to passive investment management increases the likelihood that a significant amount of investment capital will continue to flow into low-cost ETFs and mutual funds that will be more price and valuation insensitive.

- *Low call option volatility:* As discussed in much detail previously, the need for yield in a yield-starved environment resulted in a proliferation of short volatility strategies. Many of these volatility selling strategies are symmetric in their exposure to calls and puts. As discussed later, a lower implied volatility of call options requires a larger notional sale of call options, depressing the call option volatility.

- *Elevated volatility skew:* The cost of equity replacement using call options is still relatively low when the level of implied volatilities is low and the volatility skew (the difference in volatility spread between put options and call options) is elevated. The result is that call options are relatively cheaper than puts on a volatility-normalized basis.

- *Cross-market demand for convexity:* Credit products, such as high yield, cannot keep up with large rallies in the equity markets and also cannot compete with central banks crowding out private investors in the demand for corporate bonds. Because many credit investors track popular credit benchmarks, they can enhance total return by using upside convexity strategies.

Let us analyze this further: Consider an investor who is invested in high-yield credit. Credit risk as measured by credit spreads is negatively correlated to the equity of the issuing firm and positively correlated to the asset volatility of the firm via the well-known Merton model (Merton 1974). In other words, one can locally (but not globally) replicate a long position in a company's corporate bonds by buying an appropriate amount of equity in the company. To replicate larger moves in the corporate bonds requires the purchase of options. As the value of the underlying assets rises, credit spreads compress because the implicit put option in the bond price is now worth less. If the uncertainty or volatility in the company's financial prospects decreases, the value of the put also falls, compressing spreads. This suggests that in addition to having indirect exposure to the equity price, an investor holding credit also has exposure to the volatility of the underlying equity, which reflects the uncertainty in the asset prices of the company. When spreads are neither too large nor too small and the volatility of the underlying assets is not too high, credit can locally be replicated using only the underlying equity. But when asset prices either fall by larger amounts (which is accompanied by rising volatility) or rise by larger amounts, the replication of credit requires that the investor supplement the equity with explicit options. Thus, to participate in credit asset upside, call options overlaid on credit are required.

As an example, if the volatility of the traditional diffusion process is 12%, and we assume that the stock market has a 100% probability of one jump of 10%, then using just the diffusion-based Black–Scholes formula, the price of a one-year option, 5% out of the money, is approximately 2.9%. After including the 10% jump, however, the price of this same option is computed to be 4.23%, or approximately 50% higher. As another example, for a one-month horizon, the 5% out-of-the-money call option according to a jump model would cost almost four times as much if the jumps were appropriately priced, when compared to using a model with no jumps.

If "up-jumps" are not priced into the market price of options, sellers of these options might erroneously believe that they can hedge their upside exposure by trading continuously.[16] While the assumptions of the ability to dynamically hedge were found to be seriously flawed in the market crash of 1987, the dearth of equity market melt-ups still provides many participants the comfort that they can hedge their upside risk by continuous trading.

---

[16]Note that in the presence of large jumps, creating a perfect local hedge is not possible, that is, many of the assumptions of Black–Scholes are violated *ab initio*, so option prices should be expected to be higher than they would be in the absence of jumps. Assume that returns of the equity market follow a jump diffusion:

$$\frac{dS}{S} = \mu\, dt + \sigma\, dZ + J\, dq.$$

The expected log return from time t to time $t + \Delta t$ is $(\mu + J\lambda)\Delta t$, where λ is the density of jumps in a unit time interval (e.g., the number of jumps per year). For simplicity, we assume that the jumps are of a constant size J. In the limit that the time interval goes to zero, the variance of the jump diffusion for one large jump is $\sigma_{JD}^2 = \sigma^2 + J^2\lambda$, that is, jumps increase the volatility of the underlying process. In the jump-diffusion framework, the price of a call option is the weighted sum of call options with zero to many jumps, with the weighting equal to the Poisson probability of observing that many jumps. The price of a call option C_{JD} is the expected payoff weighted by the number of jumps:

$$C_{JD} = e^{-rT}\sum_{n=0}^{\infty}\frac{(\lambda T)^n}{n!}e^{-\lambda T}E\Big[\max\big(S_T^n - K, 0\big)\Big].$$

The jump formula for a call option can be written in terms of a weighted average of Black–Scholes options prices C_{BS} as

$$C_{JD} = e^{-\lambda t}\sum_{n=0}^{\infty}\frac{(\lambda t)^n}{n!}C_{BS}(S, K, t, \sigma, r_n).$$

Here, $r_n = r - \lambda(e^J - 1) + \dfrac{nJ}{t}$ is the compensated drift to account for risk neutrality.

83

This belief has resulted in the asymmetric index option skew. The put–call pricing asymmetry is reflected in the relative pricing of options and therefore in the implied volatilities corresponding to different strikes.

For example, the Credit Suisse Fear Barometer measures investor sentiment for a three-month horizon by pricing a "zero-cost" collar (selling an upside call to purchase a downside put). The Fear Barometer represents the strike of an out-of-the-money put that can be bought by selling a 10% out-of-the-money call. If the value of the Fear Barometer falls, this implies that the strike of the put that can be purchased is closer to being at the money (i.e., that the market "feels" less fearful). In other words, the volatility skew can be interpreted as the extra premium a seller of the option requires to mitigate the risk that he might not be able to hedge his risk by trading in the underlying.[17]

The equation that shows the hedge ratio illustrates why melt-ups in the markets might result in a feedback loop from the destabilizing influence of options-based hedging. This situation became newsworthy toward the end of 2020 (Peterseil, Griefeld, and Barnert 2020). In particular, because call option volatility has been very low for an extended period of time, the destabilizing

---

[17]To address how up-jumps affect the volatility skew, let us assume that the risk-free rate is zero and there is only one large jump of size J. Then, with a current index price of S and a small probability p of an up-jump and probability $1 - p$ of a small down move D, risk neutrality requires

$$S = p(S + J) + (1 - p)(S - D),$$

that is,

$$D = \frac{p}{1-p} J \sim pJ.$$

If we assume that $p \ll \sigma\sqrt{t} \ll J/S$ (i.e., the jump probability is much smaller than the diffusion volatility and the percentage size of the up-jump), then close to at the money, the price of a call option with strike K under jump diffusion with only one jump is given by

$$C_{JD} \approx C_{BS}(S,\sigma) + pJ\left(\frac{1}{2} - \frac{1}{\sigma\sqrt{(2\pi t)}}\ln\left(\frac{S}{K}\right)\right).$$

The risk to an option market maker emanates from the mistake in estimating the "gamma" of an option between the jump-based model and the Black–Scholes model. This is derived by taking the second derivative of the option prices with respect to the underlying and equals

$$\frac{\partial^2 C_{JD}}{\partial S^2} - \frac{\partial^2 C_{BS}}{\partial S^2} = \frac{Jp}{\sqrt{(2\pi t)}S^2\sigma}.$$

So, when volatility is low, the gamma or the rate of change of delta of the option priced under jumps will be much larger than the option priced under Black–Scholes. If the product of the jump magnitude and probability increases, the gamma increases rapidly.

influence of call options could likely be significant. If many participants are hedging their call options using Black–Scholes and a sharp increase occurs in the likelihood of a large upward jump, then the need for extra hedging can rapidly propel the underlying market higher, as has been observed recently in the S&P 500, NASDAQ, and many tech and "meme" stocks, such as Tesla (TSLA) GameStop (GME), and AMC Entertainment (AMC).

How much do these jumps affect the volatility? To translate the result into Black–Scholes volatility, we can set the jump price of the call to its Black–Scholes price with a volatility Σ:

$$C_{JD} = C_{BS}(S,\Sigma) \approx C_{BS}(S,\sigma) + (\partial C_{BS}/\partial \sigma)(\Sigma - \sigma).$$

Solving this equation, the adjusted volatility that needs to be plugged into Black–Scholes to recover the effect of the skew is

$$\Sigma = \sigma + \frac{pJ}{S\sqrt{t}}\left(\sqrt{\frac{\pi}{2}} + \frac{1}{\sigma\sqrt{t}}\ln\left(\frac{K}{S}\right) \right).$$

Here are some observations from this result:

- *"Spot Up, Vol Up":* As the probability of an up-jump or the size of a jump increases, the volatility increases as a function of the product of the jump probability and the jump magnitude. If a large positive shock is expected as a result of increased probability of the shocks, volatility will increase very rapidly if p and J are positively correlated. This phenomenon is typically called "spot up, volatility up" because it implies a rise in implied volatility as the markets rally and has been considered anomalous since the 1987 crash. We see that with large positive jumps, the result is not all that surprising and indeed is what was seen in 2020 in many tech company stock options.

- *Impact on Term Structure of Skew:* As S increases, or the time t to expiry increases, the jump-adjusted volatility falls. So, the jump risk is a major risk for shorter-dated options and less so as the horizon increases. As an insurance policy, shorter-dated call options are thus likely to be more responsive to jump risks. Sudden, unexpected positive shocks can then create rapid, short-term changes in the volatility smile.

- *Effect of Low-Volatility Environment:* When the volatility is low (i.e., σ is small), the correction to the Black–Scholes volatility from jumps is larger than when the volatility is already at a high level. In other words, the potential for upside dislocation and need for upside hedges is more pronounced when starting from low volatility levels, such as those that prevail today. Because central banks' action in the markets targets (lower) volatility, call options become more attractive. Increased negative gamma makes delta-hedging risk more acute on the upside.

The Rise of Digital Currencies

A major development since the original 2010 white paper on bitcoin is the digital currency's emergence at significant scale and investors' participation in it. Its volatility and stratospheric rise in price has astounded most market participants, and some have called it an event as important as the invention of paper money many centuries ago (**Exhibit 19**).

That the emergence and exponential growth of digital currencies such as bitcoin has coincided with low and negative interest rates and massive money printing and asset purchases by global central banks could simply be a coincidence. But it also could be a rational, asymmetric reflection of the reaction against fiat currency and the willingness and ability of governments to debase their currencies. As we know, currency has three main roles: a store of value, a medium of transaction, and an instrument to implement monetary policy.

Exhibit 19. Price of Bitcoin 2010–2020

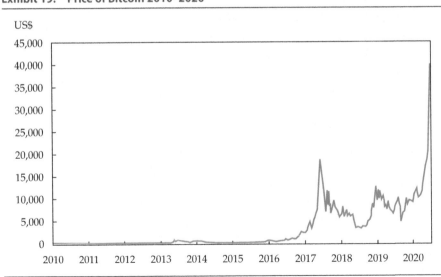

Note: All dates as of 19 July.
Source: Bloomberg Finance L.P. (XBT).

As discussed in the chapter on central banks, we know that interest rates are tightly linked to the supply of money in the system.

Interest rates have therefore been used as a tool to influence monetary policy. In a world where cryptocurrency can coexist with traditional currency, such monetary policy becomes less potent because the interest rates set by the central bank of one country do not necessarily apply to a cryptocurrency whose supply is not regulated by any one central bank. In late 2020 and early 2021, many well-known institutional fund managers pivoted from ridiculing bitcoin to openly embracing it. Because only 21 million bitcoin can ever be printed, the demand for the limited amount of bitcoin seems to have created most of the increase in price.

There has been talk recently of CBDC (central bank digital currency) that might actually serve all three roles of currency. However, the possibility of central banks being able to force negative interest rates on digital currency will likely not be very popular because this would allow for the possibility of a central bank essentially confiscating the value of money from ordinary investors through fiat. However, once negative interest rates have run their course as a mechanism to redistribute wealth, we should expect CBDCs to be one potent tool that policymakers would push forward as a replacement for private digital assets.

7. Conclusion: Is There Really Anything Wrong with Negative Yields?

> We seem to have a compulsion these days to bury time capsules in order to give those people living in the next century or so some idea of what we are like. I have prepared one of my own. I have placed some rather large samples of dynamite, gunpowder, and nitroglycerin. My time capsule is set to go off in the year 3000. It will show them what we are really like.
>
> *—Alfred Hitchcock*

As I was writing this monograph, the world continued to change at an increasingly rapid pace. More countries have cut rates into negative territory, with the US Fed now one of the few central banks still holding out. Will it go negative? When and how will that actually happen? Or will inflation become the next major problem?

The shock of COVID-19 has created a path-dependent evolution of global economies and financial markets. As always, interest rates and bond yields might be buffeted by natural disasters, wars, pandemics, and new doctrines, but it seems appropriate to conclude that "there is more continuity in interest rates than there is in most prices. This is because the interest rate is a ratio of like to like. Like rates produce the same mathematical result in any era, in any currency, and at any given price structure" (Homer and Sylla 2005).

What can we conclude about the current state of the bond markets after this wide-ranging discussion of negative interest rates and bond yields? Here is a short summary of this monograph:

- As long as there is some need to defer consumption and institutional justification for holding bonds that goes beyond their return-generating attributes, demand for negative-yielding bonds from various sectors may remain high (see Chapter 4: Who Buys Negative-Yielding Bonds, and Why?).

- Negative interest rates allow for a convenient convergence of monetary and fiscal policy. In the final analysis, monetary and fiscal powers are granted to government authorities, and when fiscal policy is ineffective, monetary policy has to take up the slack by taxing and "lending" rather than taxing and "spending," via the mechanism of negative interest rates (see Chapter 5: The Central Role of Central Banks).

- Because bond yields are so fundamental to asset valuation and risk, the impact of negative yields goes far beyond the fixed-income markets and affects all aspects of markets. In particular, low-yielding bonds affect equity markets and possibly create amplification that could result in more frequent booms and busts and financial instability. The economic consequences of these cycles lead to further government action via monetary and fiscal policy (see Chapter 6: Consequences for Asset Allocation and Risk Management). This means that the potential for loss and profit in finance is alive and well.

Only time will tell whether the great economic experiment of this generation (i.e., negative yields in the bond markets) was successful in generating desired economic outcomes. As usual, financial market participants and profit seekers are way ahead of academia in adjusting to the consequences of such unprecedented policy. Dogmas change. In the 1970s, sugar was being advertised as a diet aid (Garber 2015). Is the "sugar" of negative interest rates actually healthy for the economy? Only time, new research, and the benefit of hindsight will tell.

What about risks? The sheer size of what would traditionally be considered an anomaly has the potential to create substantial distortions across markets and strategies. A disorderly unwind of many of these policies, whether due to political or market reasons, can be substantially disruptive. The lesson for market participants is straightforward: Those who are looking to global bond markets for long-term positive returns at current levels of risk and reward, or even diversification, are likely to be disappointed if and when government backstop for these markets is removed (which, of course, is not predictable). Market participants who are looking to the bond markets for insurance against catastrophic deflation, default, or geopolitical troubles are likely to be able to justify owning bonds with negative yields in the short run because these high-priced bonds are essentially options against catastrophic loss of capital. Even so, they should really evaluate whether other methods are available to insure against such losses. From the perspective of risk premium harvesters, the conclusion is even more straightforward: Perhaps for the first time in recent memory, a long-term investor may earn a risk premium not by buying bonds but by doing the exact opposite because a bond sold at a premium price today will pull down to par at maturity!

At the end of the day, negative rates bring fiscal and monetary policy closer together and thereby serve the objectives of governments. One can ask whether negative rates are anything more than a transfer of wealth from savers to borrowers and, if so, what this wealth redistribution achieves that taxation cannot. If we imagine a world in which the central banks create digital dollars, what stops them from reaching into the phones in our pockets and taking some of the digital savings, either through direct confiscation, taxation, or just negative interest? The convergence of monetary and fiscal policy with the predilection of governments to spend beyond their capacity is nothing new in history and is not always bad, given that the government has the critical role of stepping in where private participants refuse to or cannot step.

But this convergence has social repercussions. A photomontage of former ECB president Mario Draghi in the German newspaper *Bild* had this to say about negative interest rates: "Count Draghila is sucking our accounts dry." Italy benefited from this wealth transfer and might have a very different perspective (notably, in February 2021, Draghi was appointed prime minister of Italy).

An increasingly loud chorus of people is asserting that low and negative interest rates are increasing inequality. As the Fed slashed interest rates to zero in 2020 and Congress passed massive fiscal stimulus bills, asset owners saw their wealth rise to record levels on the back of a stock market rally.

If low interest rates result in an increase in asset prices, we could naturally assume that those who are wealthier and own assets will disproportionately see their wealth increase. In Europe, because of a singular interest rate policy for all countries, regions that have higher exposure to asset prices are also likely to do better, as are poorer countries that need easier financial conditions (Hauptmeier, Holm-Hadulla, and Nikalexi 2020). As this manuscript is being written, gross nonfinancial corporate debt is reaching record highs, margin loans to buy equity have made new records, corporate bond yields have seen record lows, and the size of the balance sheet of central banks has reached a new record of almost US$25 trillion. The purportedly positive virtuous cycle of money printing, low yields, and high returns (but not high *expected* returns) seems to have no end.

Modern Monetary Theory, which holds that a sovereign with a printing press can print an unlimited amount of money to solve economic and social problems, is now treated as mainstream doctrine by central bankers, though most economists would not call it mainstream in any way. For now, most asset owners and debtors are not complaining because they feel wealthier. How investment managers and policymakers deal with the consequences of inflation and yields, if they should ever rise sharply, remains to be seen. For now, negative yields make borrowing essentially free and reduce debt servicing costs effectively to zero for many countries, despite the massive amount of debt principal. If yields were ever to rise, could a sharply higher debt service burden become impossible to manage without suffering a run on the currency and credit of these sovereign issuers?

How policy deals with social opinion will also, in the long run, determine whether these experimental and uncharted policies are allowed to run their full course or be terminated prematurely. The results in either case, like those of any experiment, are far from known as of this writing.

To me, as an observer, participant, and curious person at heart, these circumstances make the present a great time to be in the financial markets. There are many more questions to be answered each day, and the answers to these questions are not readily available in history.

Afterword: Between Here and the Long Run

The global political economy is evolving a new social and financial architecture—led by reascendancy of sovereign governments' great fiscal power, harnessed to fiat monetary creation—to guide the invisible hand of private market capitalism.

In many ways, sovereign governments are rediscovering the great wisdom of John Maynard Keynes (1936):

> Speculators may do no harm as bubbles on a steady stream of enterprise. But the position is serious when enterprise becomes the bubble on a whirlpool of speculation. When the capital development of a country becomes a by-product of the activities of a casino, the job is likely to be ill-done. (p. 142)

This unfolding transformation, accelerated by the COVID-19 pandemic, is nowhere more profound, and obvious, than in global financial markets, which are rebooting to a world in which fiscal policy is reasserting its dominance over monetary policy, in the pursuit of both macroeconomic stabilization and outcomes that pass a smell test of inclusive growth and social justice.

Simply put, central banks are losing their status as the putative only game in town in the political economy.

Sovereign governments are relearning the verity that central banks are their own creation and should be harnessed to maximize the collective welfare of their citizenry, serving as the handmaiden of fiscal policy rather than the disciplinarian of fiscal policy.

In the proverbial long run, this structural pivot to dominance of fiscal policy over monetary policy will be reflationary for wages as well as for goods and services prices on Main Street.

Paradoxically, however, the journey to that long run of more-just economic outcomes for Main Street will include an interregnum of hyperinflation risk in asset prices on Wall Street.

Understanding the dynamics of this interregnum is what Vineer's excellent treatise is all about, articulating what I call an "N + 1 system," in which the private financial sector increasingly becomes a captive "N" and sovereign-guided central banks become the ever more forceful "1."

Or put differently, it is an interlude in which Wall Street becomes a taker, rather than a maker, of its valuation architecture—one that serves a broader purpose than the pursuit of private profit.

To be sure, the name of the game on Wall Street will remain one of arbitraging relative price valuations—as it should be, providing the illusion of liquidity for all, the mother's milk of animal-spirited risk-taking, the genius of capitalism's wonder-working power of prosperity.

But the parameters of that process of creative destruction will increasingly be shaped by sovereign governments, rather than Wall Street itself, most notably in central banks' shaping of the entire term structure for sovereign debt yields, the benchmark for all private sector asset valuations.

The Occam's razor punchline is this: The putative bond market vigilantes of old are dead.

They have been forced to throw down their swords and are now rationally allying with the will of sovereign governments, representing the will of their peoples to use the power of fiat money to enhance the general welfare.

The severity and longevity of this interregnum of hyperinflation risk in asset prices will be a function of how long it takes sovereign governments to fully embrace the democratic imperative of redeploying the helicopters of fiat money creation directly to the citizenry.

Between here and there, the mode of asset price distributions on Wall Street will be up, but the tails of the distribution will grow ever fatter.

Paul McCulley

Bibliography

Agarwal, Ruchir, and Miles S. Kimball. 2019. "Enabling Deep Negative Rates to Fight Recessions: A Guide." IMF Working Paper 19/84 (April).

Akerlof, George, and Robert Shiller. 2009. *Animal Spirits: How Human Psychology Drives the Economy, and Why It Matters for Global Capitalism.* Princeton, NJ: Princeton University Press.

Alchian, Armen A., and Benjamin Klein. 1973. "On a Correct Measure of Inflation." *Journal of Money, Credit and Banking* 5 (1): 173–91.

Appelbaum, Binyamin. 2019. *The Economists' Hour: False Prophets, Free Markets, and the Fracture of Society.* New York: Little, Brown and Company.

Appell, Douglas. 2019. "Classification Change by Japan's GPIF Paves the Way for Further Boost in Foreign Bond Allocations." *Pensions & Investments* (1 October). https://www.pionline.com/markets/classification-change-japans-gpif-paves-way-further-boost-foreign-bond-allocations.

Arrata, William, Benoit Nguyen, Imene Rahmouni-Rousseau, and Miklos Vari. 2018. "The Scarcity Effect of Quantitative Easing on Repo Rates: Evidence from the Euro Area." IMF Working Paper 18/258 (December).

Bartsch, Elga, Jean Boivin, Stanley Fischer, and Philipp Hildebrand. 2019. "Dealing with the Next Downturn: From Unconventional Monetary Policy to Unprecedented Policy Coordination." BlackRock Investment Institute, Macro and Market Perspectives (August).

Bassetto, Marco, and Thomas J. Sargent. 2020. "Shotgun Wedding: Fiscal and Monetary Policy." *Annual Review of Economics* (12): 659–90.

Bhansali, Vineer. 2007. "Volatility and the Carry Trade." *Journal of Fixed Income* 17 (3): 72–84.

———. 2011. *Bond Portfolio Investing and Risk Management.* New York: McGraw-Hill.

———. 2014. *Tail Risk Hedging: Creating Robust Portfolios for Volatile Markets.* New York: McGraw-Hill.

———. 2018. "Right Tail Hedging: Managing Risk When Markets Melt Up." *Journal of Portfolio Management* 44 (7): 55–62.

———. 2019. "What a Thirty-One Year Negatively Yielding Zero Coupon Bund Means for Investors." *Forbes* (23 August). https://www.forbes.com/sites/vineerbhansali/2019/08/23/what-a-thirty-one-year-negatively-yielding-zero-coupon-bund-means-for-investors/?sh=607f0e476c6a.

Bhansali, Vineer, Matthew P. Dorsten, and Mark B. Wise. 2009. "Asymmetric Monetary Policy and the Yield Curve." *Journal of International Money and Finance* 28 (8): 1408–25.

Bhansali, Vineer, and Larry Harris. 2018. "Everybody's Doing It: Short Volatility Strategies and Shadow Financial Insurers." *Financial Analysts Journal* 74 (2): 12–23.

Bianco, Jim. 2019. "Negative Rates Threaten the Financial System." *Bloomberg Opinion* (3 September). https://www.bloomberg.com/opinion/articles/2019-09-03/negative-interest-rates-threaten-the-financial-system.

BIS. 2019. "Claudio Borio's Remarks." *BIS Quarterly Review* (September). https://www.bis.org/publ/qtrpdf/r_qt1909_ontherecord.htm?mc_cid=e89cb9e613&mc_eid=092886b7fe.

Board of Governors of the Federal Reserve System. 2020a. *Financial Stability Report* (May). https://www.federalreserve.gov/publications/files/financial-stability-report-20200515.pdf.

———. 2020b. *Financial Stability Report* (November). https://www.federalreserve.gov/publications/files/financial-stability-report-20201109.pdf.

Booth, Danielle DiMartino. 2017. *Fed Up: An Insider's Take on Why the Federal Reserve Is Bad for America*. New York: Penguin Random House.

Brunnermeier, Markus K., and Yann Koby. 2018. "The Reversal Interest Rate." NBER Working Paper No. 25406 (December).

Buiter, Willem. 2009. "Negative Nominal Interest Rates: Three Ways to Overcome the Zero Lower Bound." *North American Journal of Economics and Finance* 20 (3): 213–238.

Cameron, William Bruce. 1963. *Informal Sociology: A Casual Introduction to Sociological Thinking*. New York: Random House.

Campbell, Donald T. 1979. "Assessing the Impact of Planned Social Change." *Evaluation and Program Planning* 2 (1): 67–90.

Citi Equity Research. 2019. *De-Equitisation: Why Markets Are Shrinking and What It Means*. Citibank Research Global Strategy Team.

Cunningham, Lawrence A., ed. 2019. *The Essays of Warren Buffett: Lessons for Corporate America*. Durham, NC: Carolina Academic Press.

Darracq Pariès, Matthieu, Christoffer Kok, and Matthias Rottner. 2020. "Reversal Interest Rate and Macroprudential Policy." European Central Bank Working Paper No. 2487 (November).

Davies, Paul J. 2019. "Oxymoron Alert: Some 'High Yield' Bonds Go Negative." *Wall Street Journal* (14 July). https://www.wsj.com/articles/oxymoron-alert-some-high-yield-bonds-go-negative-11563096601.

———. 2021. "Europe's COVID-19 Bond Issuance Addressed Fiscal Shortcomings." *Wall Street Journal* (2 January).

Eggertsson, Gauti B., Ragnar E. Juelsrud, and Ella Getz Wold. 2017. "Are Negative Nominal Interest Rates Expansionary?" NBER Working Paper No. 24039 (November).

El-Erian, Mohamed A. 2016. *The Only Game in Town: Central Banks, Instability, and Avoiding the Next Collapse*. New York: Random House.

European Central Bank. 2014. "The ECB's Negative Interest Rate." European Central Bank website (12 June). https://www.ecb.europa.eu/explainers/tell-me-more/html/why-negative-interest-rate.en.html.

———. 2019. "Introductory Statement, Mario Draghi, President of the ECB." Press conference (12 September). https://www.ecb.europa.eu/press/pressconf/2019/html/ecb.is190912~658eb51d68.en.html.

———. 2020. "Survey of Professional Forecasters Q1 2020." Accessed 24 January 2020. https://www.ecb.europa.eu/stats/ecb_surveys/survey_of_professional_forecasters/html/ecb.spf2020q1~daa5609f81.en.html.

European Commission. n.d. "SURE: The European Instrument for Temporary Support to Mitigate Unemployment Risks in an Emergency." https://ec.europa.eu/info/business-economy-euro/economic-and-fiscal-policy-coordination/financial-assistance-eu/funding-mechanisms-and-facilities/sure_en.

Fitzgerald, Maggie. 2019. "Greenspan Says 'There Is No Barrier' to Negative Yields in the US." CNBC (13 August).

Friedman, Milton. 1970. *Counter-Revolution in Monetary Theory*. Wincott Memorial Lecture, Institute of Economic Affairs, Occasional paper 33.

Garber, Megan. 2015. "If Sugar Is Fattening, How Come So Many Kids Are Thin?" *The Atlantic* (19 June). https://www.theatlantic.com/entertainment/archive/2015/06/if-sugar-is-fattening-how-come-so-many-kids-are-thin/396380/.

Geisst, Charles R. 2013. *Beggar Thy Neighbor: A History of Usury and Debt.* Philadelphia: University of Pennsylvania Press.

Goodhart, Charles. 1981. "Problems of Monetary Management: The UK Experience." In *Inflation, Depression and Economic Policy in the West,* edited by Anthony S. Courakis, 111–46. Washington, DC: Rowman & Littlefield Publishers.

Gygli, Savina, Florian Haelg, Niklas Potrafke, and Jan-Egbert Sturm. 2019. "The KOF Globalisation Index—Revisited." *Review of International Organizations* 14: 543–74.

Hauptmeier, Sebastian, Fédéric Holm-Hadulla, and Katerina Nikalexi. 2020. "Monetary Policy and Regional Inequality." European Central Bank Working Paper No. 2385 (March).

Hoffman, Boris, Marco J. Lombardi, Benoît Mojon, and Athanasios Orphanides. 2020. "Fiscal-Monetary Policy Interactions in a Low Interest Rate World." BIS.

Homer, Sidney. 1963. *A History of Interest Rates,* 1st ed. New Brunswick, NJ: Rutgers University Press.

Homer, Sidney, and Richard Sylla. 2005. *A History of Interest Rates,* 4th ed. Hoboken, NJ: John Wiley & Sons.

Hunter, Michael. 2019. "Even Greece Is Getting Paid to Borrow Money in Debt Markets." *Bloomberg* (9 October). https://www.bloomberg.com/news/articles/2019-10-09/greece-draws-negative-yield-for-first-time-in-3-month-bill-sale.

Keynes, John Maynard. 1936. *The General Theory of Employment, Interest, and Money.* New York: Harcourt, Brace and Company.

Kocherlakota, Narayana. 2020. "The Fed Should Go Negative Next Week." *Bloomberg Opinion* (4 April).

Koranyi, Balazs, and Francesco Canepa. 2020. "ECB 'Undeterred' by German Court Ruling over Bond Buying." Reuters (7 May). https://www.reuters.com/article/us-ecb-policy-deguindos-idUSKBN22J0V7.

Laskow, Sarah. 2016. "The Most Beautiful Tulip in History Cost as Much as a House." *Atlas Obscura* (28 April). https://www.atlasobscura.com/articles/the-most-beautiful-tulip-in-history-cost-as-much-as-a-house.

Lee, Yen Nee. 2019. "Long-Term Negative Rates Have 'Adverse Consequences' We Don't Fully Understand, Says Jamie Dimon." CNBC (21 October, updated 22 October). https://www.cnbc.com/2019/10/22/jamie-dimon-on-negative-interest-rates-economic-slowdown-recession.html.

Lockett, Hudson, and Thomas Hale. 2020. "China's First Negative-Yielding Sovereign Bond Spurs Investor Rush." *Financial Times* (18 November). https://www.ft.com/content/c02a8184-5c9d-45ce-b4bd-02b028de7f63.

Lonergan, Eric. 2014. *Money*. New York: Routledge.

Mankiw, Gregory. 2009. "It May Be Time for the Fed to Go Negative." *New York Times* (18 April). https://www.nytimes.com/2009/04/19/business/economy/19view.html.

McCormick, Liz. 2019. "Greenspan Sees No Barriers to Prevent Negative Treasury Yields." Bloomberg (13 August). https://www.bloomberg.com/news/articles/2019-08-13/greenspan-sees-no-barriers-to-prevent-negative-treasury-yields.

Merton, Robert C. 1974. "On the Pricing of Corporate Debt: The Risk Structure of Interest Rates." *Journal of Finance* 29 (2): 449–70.

Minenna, Marcello, Giovanna Maria Boi, and Paolo Verzella. 2016. *The Incomplete Currency: The Future of the Euro and Solutions for the Eurozone*. Hoboken, NJ: Wiley.

Muller, Jerry. 2018. *The Tyranny of Metrics*. Princeton, NJ: Princeton University Press.

Papoutsi, Melina, and Lira Mota. 2021. "Understanding the Effects of Unconventional Monetary Policy on Corporate Bond Market in the Euro Area." Paper presented at the 2021 American Economic Association annual meeting, Monetary Policy I paper session (4 January).

Peterseil, Yakob, Katherine Griefeld, and Jan-Patrick Barnert. 2020. "Tech Traders Say Options Hedging Is Firing Up Rally in Nasdaq." *Bloomberg* (1 September). https://www.bloomberg.com/news/articles/2020-09-01/nasdaq-volatility-twist-prompts-theories-on-storm-in-tech-stocks.

Prins, Nomi. 2018. *Collusion: How Central Banks Rigged the World*. New York: Bold Type Books.

Rasmus, Jack. 2017. *Central Bankers at the End of Their Rope?: Monetary Policy and the Coming Depression.* Atlanta: Clarity Press.

Regnier, John. 2019. "The Logic Behind the Bonds That Eat Your Money." *Bloomberg Businessweek* (24 July).

Richter, Wolf. 2019. "Negative-Yielding Junk Bonds Have Arrived in Europe." *Wolf Street* (9 July). https://wolfstreet.com/2019/07/09/negative-yielding-junk-bonds-have-arrived-in-europe/.

Rogoff, Kenneth. 2020. "The Case for Deeply Negative Interest Rates." *Project Syndicate* (4 May).

Scheidel, Walter. 2018. *The Great Leveler: Violence and the History of Inequality from the Stone Age to the Twenty-First Century.* Princeton, NJ: Princeton University Press.

Strathern, Marilyn. 1997. "'Improving Ratings': Audit in the British University System." *European Review* 5 (3): 305–321.

Vaughan, Diane. 2016. *The Challenger Launch Decision: Risky Technology, Culture, and Deviance at NASA.* Chicago: University of Chicago Press.

White, James, and Victor Haghani. 2019. "Negative Interest Rates and the Perpetuity Paradox." Elm Partners (19 November). https://elmfunds.com/perpetuity-paradox.

Wise, Mark, and Vineer Bhansali. 2010. *Fixed Income Finance: A Quantitative Approach.* New York: McGraw-Hill.

Yardeni, Edward, and Joseph Abbott. 2019. *Stock Buybacks: The True Story.* Brookville, NY: YRI Press.

Disclosures

Vineer Bhansali, PhD, is the founder and chief investment officer of LongTail Alpha, LLC, an SEC registered investment adviser and a CFTC registered CTA and CPO. Any opinions or views expressed by Dr. Bhansali are solely those of Dr. Bhansali and do not necessarily reflect the opinions or views of LongTail Alpha, LLC, any of its affiliates (collectively, "LongTail Alpha"), or any other associated persons of LongTail Alpha. You should not treat any opinion expressed by Dr. Bhansali as investment advice or as a recommendation to make an investment in any particular investment strategy or investment product. Dr. Bhansali's opinions and commentaries are based on information that he considers credible but that might not constitute research by LongTail Alpha. Dr. Bhansali does not warrant the completeness or accuracy of the information on which his opinions or commentaries are based.

This publication is for illustrative and informational purposes only and does not represent an offer or solicitation with respect to the purchase or sale of any particular security, strategy, or investment product. Past performance is not indicative of future results.

Different types of investments involve varying degrees of risk, including possible loss of the principal amount invested. Therefore, it should not be assumed that future performance of any specific investment or investment strategy, or any non-investment-related content, will be profitable or prove successful. Nothing contained herein is intended to predict the performance of any investment.

Named Endowments

The CFA Institute Research Foundation acknowledges with sincere gratitude the generous contributions of the Named Endowment participants listed below.

Gifts of at least US$100,000 qualify donors for membership in the Named Endowment category, which recognizes in perpetuity the commitment toward unbiased, practitioner-oriented, relevant research that these firms and individuals have expressed through their generous support of the CFA Institute Research Foundation.

Senior Research Fellows

Financial Services Analyst Association